Wakefield Press

Anzac Biscuits

Allison Reynolds, MA (Gastronomy), is a culinary historian and a regular commentator on many aspects of food history. As gastronomer in residence at several South Australian establishments she researched the social and food history of early Adelaide. Allison's passion for tea, marmalade, food history and old cookery books continues unabated.

By the same author

Carrick Hill: Heydays of the Haywards 1940–1970
(researched and compiled by Allison Reynolds with Jill Argent,
Margaret Denton, Elizabeth Ellison and Elizabeth Rogers)

ANZAC Biscuits

The power and spirit of an everyday national icon

ALLISON REYNOLDS

Wakefield Press

16 Rose Street
Mile End
South Australia 5031
wakefieldpress.com.au

First published 2018

Copyright © Allison Reynolds, 2018

All rights reserved. This book is copyright. Apart from
any fair dealing for the purposes of private study, research,
criticism or review, as permitted under the Copyright Act,
no part may be reproduced without written permission.
Enquiries should be addressed to the publisher.

Cover designed by Liz Nicholson, designBITE
Edited by Julia Beaven, Wakefield Press, and Annette Richards
Typeset by Michael Deves, Wakefield Press

ISBN 978 1 74305 553 3

 A catalogue record for this book is available from the National Library of Australia

 Wakefield Press thanks Coriole Vineyards for continued support

For Muma,
thank you for encouraging my interests in cooking from an early age and for continuing to inspire my food ideas decades later.

ANZAC DAY
Tuesday, April 25th, 1916.

Lunch given to the Australian Imperial Force
in Great Britain at the
HOTEL CECIL.

□

MENU

Fried Whiting with Lemon

Roast Beef

Roast Potatoes
French Beans
Tomatoes

Apricots and Rice

The Anzac Band will play during Lunch.
Bandmaster - Mr. CHARLES RATFORD.

First Anzac Day menu, 1916.
From the Hotel Cecil in London.
(Bethune Collection, Adelaide, South Australia)

Contents

Preface		ix
Chapter 1	Across the Seas – The Anzac connection	1
Chapter 2	The Anzac Biscuit – Who do you think you are?	7
Chapter 3	What's in a Name?	30
Chapter 4	Jaw Breakers – The Anzac wafer or tile	40
Chapter 5	Something from Home	55
Chapter 6	The Family Handwritten Recipe Book – A precious heirloom	70
Chapter 7	Who Put the Coconut in the Anzac Biscuit?	81
Chapter 8	Crispy versus Chewy – The eternal question	91
Chapter 9	Show Cooking and the Anzac Biscuit	107
Chapter 10	Keeping the Anzac Spirit Alive	116
Chapter 11	Sutton Veny to South Australia	124
Bibliography		135
Glossary		147
Acknowledgements		148
Index		152

Preface

Who would have thought that this humble sweet biscuit would mean so much to so many? To Australians and New Zealanders the Anzac biscuit is steeped in meaning and memory. The acronym ANZAC (Australian and New Zealand Army Corps) came into use when Australian and New Zealand soldiers were grouped in Egypt prior to the landing at Gallipoli in April 1915. The Gallipoli campaign has come to signify a defining moment in the history of both nations, especially the spirit of the brave diggers. It was a shared experience never to be forgotten.

In culinary history terms, while the origins of the dessert pavlova may have divided Australia and New Zealand it is 'Anzacs' (as the biscuits are affectionately known) that unite us. Australian food historian Professor Barbara Santich confirms the ownership of this well-loved snack and in correspondence she writes: 'The Anzac biscuit holds a particular significance to Australians and New Zealanders and is recognised as a distinctly national food in both countries, representative of national identity.'

By baking biscuits and posting them with other treats (sweets, cigarettes and local newspapers) to the troops, families on the home front were connected with their loved ones on the frontline. Receiving a package from home would have been a source of great comfort in the horrors of war, especially homemade goods. Whether these packages actually contained what we know as Anzac biscuits will be explored in the following chapters.

Anzac biscuits are unique – a hundred years after the First World War these biscuits are still filling family tins all year round, and in particular for Anzac Day on 25 April. Around this date, these biscuits are baked as a means of fundraising for the local RSL (Returned and Services League of Australia). However, commercial versions are always available in supermarkets with a percentage of the profits going to the RSL. Whether bought or homemade these tempting biscuits suit most occasions and can be served with a cup of tea or coffee anytime – at morning tea, tea after lunch, with afternoon tea or at the end of the day with supper.

Currently many myths and legends surround this small but powerful biscuit. The purpose of this book is to give an authoritative and reliable history of this iconic national food, not just for culinary history's sake but for all generations to come.

Chapter 1
Across the Seas
The Anzac connection

Sutton Veny Primary School, Wiltshire, England

I was just five years old when I started school at Sutton Veny. One of my earliest memories is of standing in the playground wearing my first school uniform – a cotton dress for summer, short white socks and polished Start-Rite sandals. Beside me was my twin sister Angela (all blonde curls and innocence). We watched in dismay as our mother disappeared down the High Street towards our home, and cried behind the fence.

On returning to the school from Australia in 2006 the significance of the ANZAC cemetery behind that fence held a new and deeper meaning for me. Childhood memories and Australian history were intertwined.

An ANZAC cemetery (maintained by the Commonwealth War Graves Commission) lies adjacent to the school playground in the sacred grounds of the Church of St John the Evangelist. The parish records confirm that there are 168 WWI burials, of which 143 are Australian including those of two nurses. A low dry-stone wall divides the graveyard from the playing fields, cricket pitch and pavilion. The setting is picturesque, peaceful and so typical of an English village.

My family moved two or three times in the area before finally settling a few miles away from Sutton Veny in the village of

Sutton Veny Church of England Primary School students commemorate Anzac Day. (Photographer Mrs E.J. Humphries, 2007)

Heytesbury. As children we knew about the ANZAC graves but it would be decades later that they would make such a lasting impression on me.

Older residents remember children picking flowers for the war graves. I can recall my Sunday school at the Church of St Peter and St Paul Heytesbury making annual excursions into the woods to pick the first flowers of spring so that we children could make posies to take home on Mothering Sunday. So I can well imagine that in 1918 a small group of schoolchildren would have gone into the copses around Sutton Veny, picked wild flowers and placed them on the graves of the newly buried Australian soldiers.

While it is no longer possible to pick wild flowers, the tradition of young children placing posies on the ANZAC graves continues. The flowers are donated by local florists and supermarkets and the students in their Sutton Veny school houses (Auckland, Brisbane, Canberra, Darwin, Elliston, Geraldton and Nelson), turn the flowers into posies which they place by each headstone during the school memorial service.

St John the Evangelist Church at Sutton Veny holds an annual

Anzac Day Service of Remembrance on the Sunday closest to Anzac Day. Following the service, representatives from the Australian High Commission, the Commonwealth War Graves Commission, the British Australia Society and the local British Legion lay wreaths on the Australian War Graves memorial.

The Australian and New Zealand flags are permanently on display in the dedicated ANZAC side chapel. A faded reproduction of 'Signals in Action', painted by South Australian war artist Ivor Hele and dedicated to Signals Engineers, hangs on the chapel wall, and a visitors' book is displayed indicating the many overseas visitors to Sutton Veny.

Codford – a lasting memorial

Sutton Veny is not the only ANZAC cemetery in the area. A few miles away lies the charming village of Codford. The Codford cemetery is the largest New Zealand WWI war grave cemetery in the UK and the second largest Australian cemetery after Sutton Veny. Here there are 97 ANZAC graves (66 New Zealanders and 31 Australians). The Church of Codford St Mary honours the ANZACs with a daybreak service on Anzac Day. A lone piper leads the congregation down Church Lane to the village hall for a full English 'gunfire' breakfast; the 'gunfire' in question being the Australian rum added to the tea or coffee. It is said that rum was added to the tea before the troops began the landings at Suvla Bay in Turkey.

During 1916 the Australians left a lasting reminder in Wiltshire by carving the Australian Imperial Forces (AIF) Army badge into the chalk hillside above Foxhill Bottom at Lamb Down on the outskirts of Codford, beside the very busy and hazardous A36 road. (It is much safer to view the 175-foot-wide by 150-foot-tall badge from the nearby village of Stockton.) Regular travellers between Salisbury and Warminster look out for this famous landmark – the Rising Sun badge – from the safety of the train. Soldiers pushed the ends of green, brown and clear beer bottles into the carving so that from a distance the badge glistened in the sun and shone like bronze. For security reasons the badge was covered over during WWII and later became overgrown and hardly noticed. Nowadays, local army

Chalk Army badge of the Australian Imperial Forces, Lamb Down, Codford, Wiltshire. (Author's photograph, 2014)

personnel and villagers carry out an annual clean up of the Codford badge.

We had often wondered why so many ANZACs were buried in our Wiltshire villages. The location of Sutton Veny and Codford (in close proximity to Warminster, Salisbury Plain and a main rail line) made these villages ideally placed to create army camps and training grounds for the troops prior to their deployment to northern France.

The 26th Division was stationed at Sutton Veny in 1915. In 1916 the No. 1 Australian Command Depot moved to Sutton Veny where it remained until 1919. After the Armistice the No. 1 Australian General Hospital was transferred to Sutton Veny where it stayed until the end of 1919. The No. 3 New Zealand General Hospital was based in Codford. After the horrors of the battlefield, soldiers were brought to the safety of these quiet villages for recuperation and convalescence. Sadly, many succumbed to their wounds while others were struck down by the Spanish flu pandemic which hit the area in 1918. This explains why these ANZAC soldiers and nurses were buried here in Wiltshire, so far from home.

Decades later – Anzac biscuits take me back to Sutton Veny
Between 2003 and 2013 I regularly appeared on radio 891 ABC Adelaide's 'Afternoons with Carole Whitelock' to discuss food-related stories. In 2007 I was in the UK over Anzac Day and I was able to organise a live connection to the programme and to introduce South Australian 891 listeners to the Sutton Veny/Anzac connection. Before leaving Australia, I had contacted Sutton Veny School and the head teacher (school principal in Australia) happily agreed to my suggestion of baking Anzac biscuits with the children in their classroom. I was then invited to attend the school Anzac Day service the next day, followed by afternoon tea in the village hall where the children proudly served their Anzac biscuits. This turned out to be a special year. During the service, the school Anzac co-ordinator Nicky Barnard read a letter to the congregation from the then Prime Minister of Australia, John Howard. Ms Maureen Rice of Barnstaple had sent him a newspaper clipping from the *Western Daily Press* of

26 April 2006 showing students participating in the Anzac Day service. In his message John Howard wrote of the enduring Anzac legacy, thanked the students for honouring the memory of the original ANZACs and reiterated the close association between Australia and England.

On trips back to the UK my brother David (who now lives in Melbourne) and I always visit Heytesbury, the village where we grew up, and these days we include the nearby villages of Sutton Veny and Codford. We appreciate the Anzac connection. The wire fencing around the perimeter of Sutton Veny school grounds still looks the same; it's high and intimidating – I can see why it's a memory I can't erase.

Drawing of Anzac Graves, Church of Codford St Mary, Wiltshire.
(Artist Frankie Woods, 2014)

Chapter 2
The Anzac Biscuit
Who do you think you are?

During the 19th and 20th centuries Australia and New Zealand received migrants from Great Britain who brought with them their baking heritage and cooking skills. For many years, the accepted wisdom has been that the Anzac biscuit's origins lie with the Scottish oatcake and that the recipe came with these early settlers from Great Britain. This association with Scotland is just one of the many myths and legends surrounding the Anzac biscuit still perpetuated today.

It was understandable that this connection was made because we know that Scottish people were renowned for their baking prowess. The major ingredient in both of these recipes is oats, albeit in the form of oatmeal in oatcakes and rolled oats or oat flakes in Anzac biscuits. The fact that neither recipe included eggs may have contributed to this thinking.

In *Bold Palates: Australia's Gastronomic Heritage*, Australian food historian Dr Barbara Santich found no 'obvious ancestor' of the Anzac biscuit. Santich argues that 'British tradition provides no direct antecedent, though Anzacs borrow some features of both gingerbread and parkin'.

The major feature that gingerbreads and parkins share with the Anzac biscuit is the method by which they are made. This method is a cooking technique known as 'the melting method', which we will investigate later in this chapter.

Before examining similar biscuit recipes it is important to understand the significance of the method of making, the finishing technique and the ingredients used – all these factors contribute to what defines an Anzac biscuit and will also help us in our search to find its origins.

The method of making and the finishing technique

Among similar biscuit recipes, differences were found in the way ingredients were combined – in other words, the method of making or the cooking technique used. Many of the baking recipes incorporated 'rubbing in' (rubbing the butter into the flour), while some used the creaming method (beating the butter and sugar together), before the rest of the ingredients were added and the mixture was then formed into a dough.

There were differences in the finishing stages too; several biscuit recipes required the dough to be rolled out and then cut into shapes, whereas the Anzac biscuit method is quicker, not just in the method of making but also in the finishing techniques – as explained below.

The method of making Anzac biscuits

Anzac biscuits are made by the melting method; it is very quick and the equipment required is minimal: one mixing bowl, one spoon, one saucepan and a baking tray (also known as a baking sheet or slide). The dry ingredients (flour, oats and sugar) are put into a bowl and the butter and golden syrup or treacle are melted together in a pan to form a hot liquid. Bicarbonate of soda is then dissolved in boiling water and added to the liquid (the wet ingredients), to create a foaming mass. These wet ingredients are poured over the dry ingredients and everything is mixed thoroughly.

The finishing technique
From the mixture, small spoonfuls are dropped onto greased baking sheets leaving plenty of room for the biscuits to spread as they bake in the oven.

The ingredients
Recipes for Anzac biscuits found before 1925 did not include cocoanut (as coconut was then called). Early Australian cookery books show that cocoanut was available at the time and was a popular ingredient used in puddings, cakes and other biscuit recipes. Therefore, who put the coconut in the Anzac biscuit and why? This is of considerable significance and will be explored in Chapter 7.

Today the Anzac biscuit comprises:

> **Wet ingredients:** golden syrup, melted butter and bicarbonate of soda dissolved in hot water.
> **Dry ingredients:** flour, sugar, rolled oats and coconut.

The butter and golden syrup act as binding agents and add flavour.

The bicarbonate of soda, also known as baking soda or bicarb, acts as a leavening agent (raising agent) in baking. It is a chemical – an alkali that reacts with acid by effervescing, producing carbon dioxide. It is dissolved in hot water and added to the other hot 'wet ingredients' just before they are mixed into the dry.

The flour helps to bind the biscuit and is nutritious. The sugar adds sweetness; it also contributes to the crunchiness of the biscuit. The oats add extra nutrition, taste and texture. The golden syrup also binds the biscuit and provides sweetness, chewiness and preserving qualities.

With the exception of the coconut, I would suggest that the key ingredients that define Anzac biscuits are golden syrup and oats; and that is where our investigative trail continues.

Golden syrup – a key ingredient

Why the addition of golden syrup? In WWI the 'keeping quality' of Anzac biscuits was paramount and this lead to the inclusion of golden syrup and the exclusion of eggs as a means of binding the mixture together. The biscuits needed to last at least two to three months (the time it would take for packages to reach the troops by merchant ship). Using eggs in a recipe would have limited the 'shelf life'; however, there were other factors that contributed to the exclusion of eggs from the recipe. During WWI, many poultry farmers left the land to fight overseas, having a profound effect on egg production. As a consequence eggs were rationed. To create this biscuit, women would have drawn on their cooking know-how, using their knowledge of other baking recipes popular at the time. Golden syrup and butter used together created a good binding agent; golden syrup provided extra sweetness and the high sugar content also proved to be a good preservative. This biscuit recipe, combining cheap store cupboard ingredients with an easy method of making, was a winner with everyone; a nutritious biscuit, quick to make, which would last the journey and, most importantly, appeal to the 'boys' far from home.

The creative role of women during the First World War has been acknowledged by Sian Supski in an article for the *Journal of Australian Studies*. In her paper, *Anzac Biscuits – A Culinary Memorial*, Supski writes: 'Women's culinary creativity inspired the use of golden syrup and, in doing so, ensured the freshness of the biscuit when they reached their loved ones.'

As far as can be determined the use of golden syrup (earlier recipes used treacle and molasses) and the melting method technique had their origins in the British gingerbreads and parkins. These could be baked in the form of a cake or a biscuit and there were many variations of gingerbreads, cakes and biscuits found in early Australian cookery books. Parkin is explained later in this chapter.

Early Australian cookery books

The evolution of recipes (changes and additions) can be seen over time in Australian cookery books. For example, in the 1898 1st edition of *Mrs Maclurcan's Cookery Book – A Collection of Practical Recipes Specially Suitable for Australia* there is a recipe for oatmeal biscuits which uses the melting method. In the 1905 revised and enlarged 6th edition, ginger cake is added. This recipe also uses the melting method but in finishing, the dough is rolled out.

Further evidence for the popularity of cakes made by the melting method is shown by the inclusion of ten gingerbread/ ginger cake recipes and four ginger biscuit recipes in the baking chapter (and under its own section of Ginger Bread) in the 1911 1st edition of *The Kookaburra Cookery Book of Culinary and Household Recipes and Hints*.

Advertised as Australia's Mrs Beeton, Lady Hackett edited the popular Western Australian cookery book *The Australian*

Anzac Biscuits

Household Guide. This 1916 tome (3500 recipes) includes a large Biscuits section featuring many variations on the method of making the ginger biscuit. Among them ginger nuts, Sunderland gingerbread nuts, and ginger biscuits all use the melting method; ginger cookies and ginger wafers use the creamed method; while the ginger snaps and Sandford biscuits are rubbed in. There is no egg in the ginger biscuit recipe; here the binding ingredients are golden syrup and milk. Under the Cakes section, there are 10 gingerbread recipes, all of which use golden syrup or treacle, and one that does not contain eggs.

To take the origin of the Anzac biscuit further back into its culinary 'family tree' we need to investigate this melting method of cooking.

The melting method discovered in early British cookery books

This melting method can be found in Mrs Beeton's 1861 1st edition *Book of Household Management*. Beeton states that Sunderland gingerbread nuts is 'an excellent recipe'. While this recipe does not

Mrs Maclurcan's Cookery Book: A Collection of Practical Recipes, Specially Suitable for Australia, published in Townsville, 1898.
The Kookaburra Cookery Book of Culinary and Household Recipes and Hints, collected and arranged by the Committee of the Lady Victoria Buxton Girls' Club, Adelaide, 1911.
The Australian Household Guide, edited by Lady Hackett, Perth, 1916.
Mrs Beeton's Book of Household Management, first published in 1861.

include oats it does include spices (ground ginger, allspice and coriander seed) and it is made in the same manner. The spices are mixed with flour and sugar and then bound together with warm treacle and butter. Spoonfuls are placed onto buttered paper and baked in a slow oven.

Around the same time, this melting method was also practised in traditional Scottish baking recipes. One such recipe was parlies (the name given to the Scottish Parliament cake) and this, in true 'heeland' style, would be out on a limb (of the family tree) all of its own!

A Scottish tradition

In *The Taste of Britain*, parlies are described by Laura Mason and Catherine Brown as being more like a hard ginger biscuit than a cake. These food historians state that parlies were served with whisky, rum or brandy to the judges and lawmakers when they met for their midday break in Parliament Square, and they also confirm that recipes for parlies were found as far back as 1868. The authors write that while parlies are no longer made, Scottish bakers do continue the gingerbread tradition.

The author of *The Scots Kitchen: Its Lore and Recipes*, F. Marian McNeill, writes that parlies used to be sold at stalls in the streets of Edinburgh. McNeill includes a recipe for parlies that reveals the similarities to the gingerbread nuts (butter and treacle are melted and boiled before adding to flour, sugar and ginger). However, parlies are finished differently as McNeill instructs:

> Work up the paste as hot as your hands will bear it and roll out in rectangular shape... to fit a baking sheet. Mark into four-inch squares... Bake in a slow oven for about forty minutes,

when the cakes should be well risen and lightly browned. Separate the squares when soft. They will soon harden.

Towards the top of the 'family tree' – the melting recipes go back even further

If we look towards the top of the culinary tree, we find in the 5th edition of *The Cook's Oracle: Containing Receipts For Plain Cookery* (1823) two recipes in the Pastry section using the melting method: orange gingerbread and gingerbread nuts.

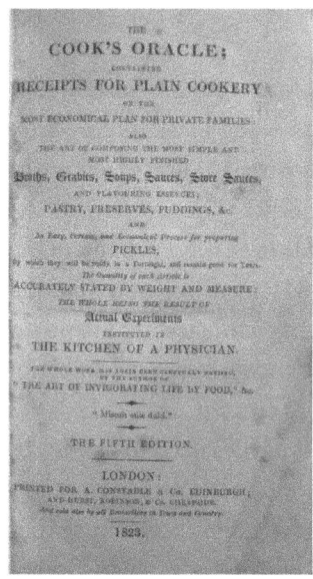

The Cook's Oracle: Containing Receipts For Plain Cookery, first published in 1822.

Both recipes have similar ingredients: fine flour, treacle, moist sugar, candied orange peel, ground ginger, allspice and butter (melted to oil).

The orange gingerbread includes additional spices (caraways and corianders mixed) and the dough is rolled out into pieces 'about the size of a small walnut', then laid in rows on a baking plate and pressed flat with the hand before baking in a slow oven. The gingerbread nuts recipe varied with the finishing method. Here the mixture is set aside for 12 hours before rolling out to half an inch thick, and being cut into pieces three inches long and two inches wide. This recipe proceeds with the instruction to 'mark them in the form of chequers with the back of a knife, put on a baking plate about a quarter of an inch apart, rub them over with a brush dipped in the Yolk of an Egg and beat up with a teacup of Milk'.

However, the most important find in this cookery book because of its similarities to the Anzac biscuit, was the handwritten recipe on the inside cover page which says, *Yorkshire "Th: hearth" Cake* and is signed: *Mrs Daly. Nov: 1854*.

"Th: hearth" Cake recipe includes oatmeal, treacle, butter, ground ginger and the rind of a lemon chopped fine. No method is given except to say that it may require more treacle, and that it should be made into cakes about the size of a small saucer and baked.

The British food author Alan Davidson writes in *The Penguin Companion to Food* that the inclusion of oatmeal in parkin gives it similarities to Grasmere gingerbread (named after a town in the English Lake District) and to the Broonie, a Scottish Orkney gingerbread. Mason and Brown add that many other British towns have gingerbread specialities that still survive today, but the recipes are closely guarded.

Going even further back, I was excited to find a recipe for gingerbread made with treacle and butter in the 1747 edition

'Yorkshire "Th: hearth" Cake. Mrs Daly. Nov: 1854' handwritten inside the cover page of *The Cook's Oracle* by M.D. William Kitchener.

of what is regarded as one of the most influential 18th century English cookery books, *The Art of Cookery Made Plain and Easy* by Hannah Glasse. Two recipes were found in the 1st edition facsimile of 1983. Ginger-Bread Cakes was a rubbed-in recipe that included nutmeg, cream and 'treakle' (sic) and then baked in a 'slack oven' (moderate heat). The other recipe on how to make ginger-bread included 'treacle', used the melting method, and was cooked in a 'quick oven' (fairly hot). It is interesting to see the two different spellings of treacle in the same edition, and the oven descriptors in the days before we had gas and electric temperature controls. (See box for references to oven temperature terminology.)

> **Oven Temperatures**
>
> Oven thermometers are discussed by Isabella Beeton in her 1861 classic, *Mrs Beeton's Book of Household Management*. She suggests approximate temperatures in Fahrenheit: 'For meat the temperature should be about 300 Fahr.; for bread 360, afterwards lowered; for pastry about the same, the richest pastry requiring the hottest oven.'
>
> Mrs Beeton also describes how to test the temperature using a piece of writing paper 'which curls up brown in a pastry oven', or with flour 'which takes every shade from coffee colour to black, when sprinkled on the floor of the oven'. And, finally she declares that 'experienced cooks test very accurately with the hand'.
>
> Prior to temperature-controlled ovens women used various words to describe suitable oven temperatures. Recipes in the baking section of the 1911 *Kookaburra Cookery Book* included some of the following words to describe the type of oven in which to bake: brisk, cool, fair, good, hot, moderate, quick, slack, slow, steady or well-heated oven.

Research on this topic has taken our trail back to the early 1700s for gingerbread recipes, in particular, those gingerbreads that include oatmeal. Before coming to our conclusion on the contenders it is necessary to look at the other key ingredient.

Oats – a key ingredient

Some early Australian cookery books contained biscuit recipes using oats, in the form of oatmeal; however, finding an actual recipe for oatcakes was more challenging. Out of the 14 cookery books examined, from 1897–1916, seven books had no similar

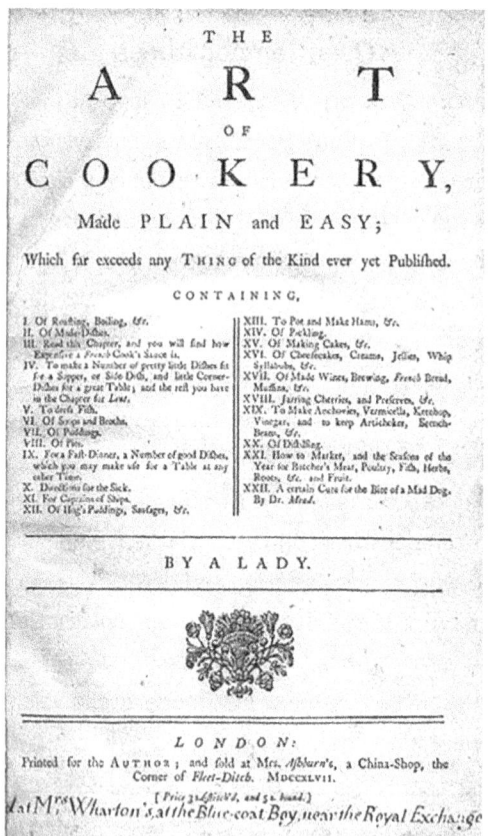

The Art of Cookery Made Plain and Easy by a Lady, **written by Hannah Glasse and first published in 1747.**

recipes to the Anzac biscuit at all, and out of the remaining seven books there were only five that contained oatmeal biscuit recipes.

The ingredients varied a little, but all oatmeal biscuit recipes included oatmeal, sugar and butter. Some recipes also added flour and egg and one recipe included ground ginger. The methods of making varied too, the butter being melted first, or creamed with the sugar, then added to the dry ingredients before turning the mixture into stiff dough. This dough was then rolled out and cut into squares before baking.

The nearest oatmeal biscuit recipe to the Anzac biscuit is taken from the 1st edition *Kookaburra Cookery Book*. This was the only recipe that used bicarbonate of soda dissolved in water; however, the butter was rubbed into the dry ingredients and golden syrup was not included. An egg was also used for binding and the instructions stated 'roll out very thin and bake in a quick oven'; slightly different ingredients and a very different finish.

A similar recipe was found for oatmeal biscuits or cakes in an 1890 British publication, *Household Cookery and Laundry Work* by Mary Black. The only differences to the *Kookaburra* recipe were the use of melted lard instead of butter, the bicarbonate of soda was mixed in with the dry ingredients, and the egg was beaten with just enough cold water 'to wet all well' before rolling.

The important factor in this recipe is that the oatmeal biscuits or cakes were made using medium, fine or super fine grades of oatmeal while Anzac biscuits use rolled oats or oat flakes. (Rolled oats/oat flakes were developed in the United States by the Quaker Oat Company in 1877.)

A staple: the grain of the region and the making of oatcakes

Oatcakes are made very differently from Anzac biscuits. According to both Laura Mason and Alan Davidson, when making Scottish oatcakes the fat is rubbed into the oatmeal and combined with water, the dough is then rolled out and cut into shapes. The main shapes are rounds and farls (triangles) or corters (quarter-circles of a large 200 mm disc). These oatcakes

A horse-drawn tram on Henley Beach, Adelaide, South Australia, showing a large advertisement along the side for Quaker Oats. (Ernest Gall, PRG, 631, Box 92/15, SLSA, circa 1898)

vary between 30 and 100 millimetres across and are 3 to 10 millimetres thick. A heavy metal plate known as a griddle ('girdle' in Scotland) is heated over a fire (or by gas or electricity) and the oatcakes are cooked on the top; once they finish cooking the oatcakes are stacked up and as they dry out they curl at the edges.

A very good description of oatcakes comes from another well-respected British food writer, Jane Grigson, in her book *English Food*:

> Oatcakes consist of oatmeal, salt and fat (dripping, bacon fat or later butter) which is 'rubbed in' and with the addition of cold water formed into soft dough. The dough is rolled out on an

oatmeal-strewn board until thin, cut into circles with a scone cutter or a dinner-plate round and then cut into quarters. The oatcakes are cooked on an ungreased medium-hot griddle without turning. After cooking oatcakes were propped up to harden besides the fire. They could be eaten either savoury with cold meat or cheese or sweet served with jam.

Apart from the Scottish oatcake, there were other baking recipes that included the ingredient oats; these recipes need to be considered when going up, down and along the 'Anzac biscuit tree'.

The other 'oat connection'

Still in the oat lineage, but taking another branch of our Anzac biscuit heritage, we shall consider the link to a form of gingerbread known as parkin that comes from Yorkshire, Lancashire and the north of England (called perkin in Northumberland and southern Scotland). Today, in UK, parkin is still a traditional food eaten on Guy Fawkes Night (also known as Bonfire Night), celebrated on 5 November.

Recipes for parkin share the other vital ingredient to be found in Anzac biscuits, the golden syrup. Before the invention of golden syrup in the 1880s, treacle or molasses would have been used. In *The Taste of Britain*, Mason writes that parkin can be like a soft sponge or a hard biscuit; the texture can vary between neighbouring areas. Both types are 'based on oatmeal, the grain of the region, mixed with flour and syrup and flavoured with ginger'.

Mason also informs us that since the 1800s some of the oatmeal has been replaced by wheat flour, the cake lightened by the addition of baking powder, and golden syrup has replaced some of the molasses. Parkin goes under a variety of names including 'moggy', the name for the sticky-textured wheat-flour parkin.

Among the 3500 recipes in *The Australian Household Guide*, Lady Hackett included a Parkin Ginger Bread recipe and a Yorkshire Parkin recipe in the Gingerbread section. Both included oatmeal.

There were parkin recipes to be found in Australian newspaper recipes too. For instance, the Useful Recipes column in the South Australian *Kapunda Herald*, 31 January 1913, included a recipe for treacle parkin. The recipe used 4 lb of the best treacle or golden syrup, 1 lb of moist brown sugar, ¾ lb of butter and ¼ lb of ground ginger. The method states 'Mix and melt all in a basin in the oven, then stir in as much oatmeal as will make the mixture stiff'.

Interestingly the recipe calls for the dough to be set aside, but goes on to give the tip of using bicarbonate of soda (an important ingredient found in Anzac biscuits) if the dough is to be baked immediately. In this recipe the instruction details are minimal – 'then bake on buttered tins in a very slow oven' – so we have no idea whether this is to take the form of a cake (as with most parkin recipes) or whether the dough is rolled and cut out or the mixture spooned out onto those buttered tins.

Another example of an early parkin recipe lacking instruction comes again from *The Kookaburra Cookery Book*. This was an overseas contribution, submitted by Mrs Bacon of Sussex. She stated it was a 'Yorkshire recipe for Bonfire Night' and listed '1 lb Scotch Oatmeal, not too fine', along with '¼ lb flour, ¼ lb butter, ¼ lb brown sugar, ½ oz ground ginger, ¼ teaspoonful carbonate of soda, 1 lb golden syrup or treacle, 1 egg and enough warm milk to mix'. No other instructions were given apart from 'bake in Yorkshire pudding tin'.

> ### A Yorkshire pudding tin
>
> A Yorkshire pudding tin is a shallow rectangular baking tin that is placed under the roasting meat to catch the beef dripping. The smoking hot dripping is then used to bake the Yorkshire pudding batter (made from eggs, milk and flour). The baked pudding (crispy and brown on the outside, soft and light on the inside) is cut into squares and was originally served on its own with gravy before the roast course (to take the edge off the appetite). Nowadays, individual portions of Yorkshire pudding are popular and these are baked in round muffin tins. In most British homes Yorkshire pudding is served with roast beef alongside roast potatoes and horseradish sauce. In some homes the batter pudding is served with any roast meats. Yorkshire pudding is considered a national dish and a significant part of the 'traditional Sunday lunch'.
>
> 'A well-buttered Yorkshire pudding-tin' was suggested by Mrs Beeton for baking the sponge cake the Victoria sandwich (named in honour of Queen Victoria). Nowadays, this popular sponge is baked in shallow, round cake tins. However, it is still sandwiched together with jam and sprinkled with castor sugar.

In early cookery books cooking skills and knowledge tend to be assumed, and most recipes had minimal instructions. They were mainly written with professional cooks in mind.

Back to the British and the birth of flapjacks

Oats are one of only four ingredients in yet another branch on our Anzac biscuit tree – the British flapjack. As far as I can tell, flapjacks are a more recent addition to the British baking repertoire and further research into British culinary history is required to confirm this theory.

Just as Australian and New Zealand children grow up making Anzacs, as a British child of the 1950s I grew up baking flapjacks. Flapjacks are not to be confused with the American pancake (also known as a flapjack) or the quite different British griddlecake or drop scone. (A drop scone is a small pancake made from a thick creamy batter and cooked on a greased griddle; they are eaten warm with butter or jam.)

British flapjacks, like Anzacs, are baked in an oven and share some of the key ingredients (oats, sugar, butter and golden syrup) – though unlike Anzacs, flapjacks do not contain flour, bicarbonate or water; and flapjacks are finished differently too.

In *The Penguin Companion to Food,* Alan Davidson describes flapjacks as follows:

> Flapjack – a term usually denoting a thick chewy biscuit made from rolled oats, sugar, butter and golden syrup baked in a flat tin. The mixture is cut into squares or fingers while still warm.

On a recent visit to UK, I was surprised to see the popularity and the variety of flapjacks now being served in British cafes, bakers' shops and tearooms. Finding a 'plain' version (just with the four main ingredients) outside of home baking is not so easy these days. Most of the flapjacks contain additional ingredients such as chocolate chips, nuts, coconut or dried fruit.

While researching Anzac biscuits I came across a recipe called

Australian flapjacks, which is the exact recipe for today's Anzac biscuit (minus the coconut). This recipe was found in a British cookery book, *Perfect Cooking: A comprehensive guide to success in the kitchen*, published by the Parkinson Stove Company Ltd. There is no publishing date for *Perfect Cooking* but the book has been identified from advertisements as being circa 1937.

The book was compiled by the senior lecturer and demonstrator Miss Gwen L. Hughes and the title page states that she held a diploma of Domestic Science at the Melbourne (Emily McPherson) College of Domestic Economy. Could it be that Miss Hughes brought the recipe with her from Australia and likened it to the British equivalent? Or, was this recipe adapted from the Anzac biscuit and then became the British flapjack? I am still to find an earlier flapjack recipe in a British cookery book.

Around the same time in Australia, the Parkinson Stove Company Ltd published *The Parkinson Cookery Book* compiled by Miss Emily Noble, who in 1937 was a cookery demonstrator for the Metropolitan Gas Company Melbourne. A recipe for Anzac biscuits (this time including coconut) appears on page 117.

Even earlier, in 1930, the 1st edition of the South Australian *School of Mines Cookery Book* was published. The joint authors were instructors of Domestic Science, (the chief instructor, Beth E. Ross, held a diploma from the Edinburgh School of Cookery and Domestic Science). On page 190 is the recipe we know as flapjacks, but in this book they are called Australian Jacks. In this recipe, butter and sugar are creamed before warm golden syrup is added along with flaked oats and salt; the mixture is pressed into a well-greased Swiss-roll tin, then baked in a moderate oven for about half an hour until golden brown. The

Perfect Cooking: A Comprehensive Guide to Success in the Kitchen by Miss Gwen L. Hughes, published in Birmingham, UK, circa 1937.
The Parkinson Cookery Book published in Melbourne, 1937.
The School of Mines Cookery Book published in Adelaide, 1930.

recipe stresses that it must be cut into strips and left until cold otherwise, if removed hot, they are liable to crumble.

Immediately after the Australian Jacks recipe, is a recipe for 'ANZACS' (as written) and interestingly this includes the usual ingredients plus cocoanut (some cookery books were still using the 'a' in the spelling) and the addition of chopped nuts.

An Australian flapjack recipe was discovered by Sue Vincent (one of my 1969 UK Catering lecturers) in her family handwritten recipe book circa 1950; it is made in the same way, using the creaming method.

What we can say is that all four of the main ingredients found in the British flapjack are also included in the Anzac biscuit. Both recipes use the melting method to combine the

The Anzac Biscuit

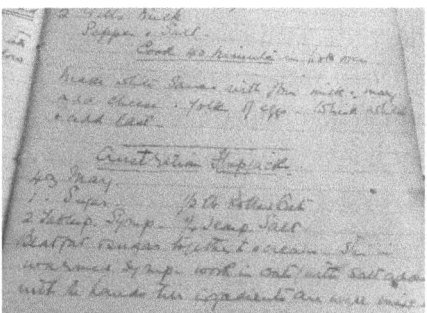 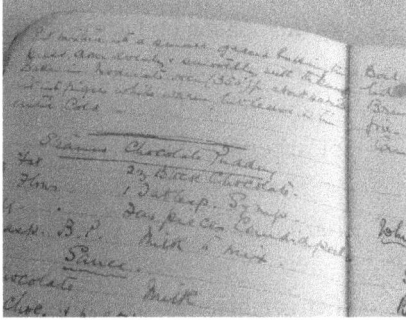

Recipe for Australian flapjacks handwritten in Sue Vincent's family recipe book, UK, circa 1950.

ingredients, but there are some differences to be found in the finishing and baking.

We now have four other biscuit/cake recipes (in addition to the Scottish oatcake) – flapjacks, parkin, ginger biscuits/gingerbreads and Scottish parlies – to consider as possible contenders as the 'ancestors' of the Anzac biscuit.

The contenders

Oatcakes Oats are the only ingredient that both recipes share (early oatcake recipes used dripping as the fat). The method of making oatcakes (rubbed in) and Anzacs (melting method) are different and there is also a difference in the finishing.

British flapjack These consist of rolled oats, sugar, butter and golden syrup, which are not quite all the ingredients (and no coconut either). Flapjacks are made by the melting method; however, it is baked whole in a tin and cut out. Finding an early British recipe has been difficult – I may yet find that the British flapjack originated from Australian Jacks!

Parkin Based on oatmeal, includes the golden syrup, sugar and butter, sometimes flour, but flavoured with ground ginger. It is also made by the melting method and sometimes includes bicarbonate of soda. Parkin can include eggs, which would make it more cake-like; if eggs are not used it would be more like a hard biscuit.

Ginger biscuits and gingerbreads All with variations – most include the golden syrup or treacle, sugar, butter, flour and bicarbonate of soda and then of course they include spices for added flavour. Some have eggs, some do not, some include fine oatmeal and most are made by the melting method. If it wasn't for the spice flavourings it would be a good link.

Scottish parlies These consist of butter, sugar, treacle, flour and ginger, a hard biscuit that is made by the melting method; however they have to be eliminated as contenders as they don't include oats. Shame it was a nice story!

Conclusion

Researching the provenance of the Anzac biscuit has led me to support Australian food historian Barbara Santich's theory that there are early British recipes with a much deeper connection to the Anzac biscuit than the Scottish oatcake. Anzac biscuits have a deeper connection to British parkin and some gingerbreads/ginger biscuits and, 'in a wee way', to Scottish parlies; they borrow a little bit from each of them, certainly far more than from the Scottish oatcakes as was previously thought. As for the British flapjack, we may yet find that like the boiled fruit cake and the iced Christmas pudding, the recipe was taken from the

Antipodes and embraced by the home country. More research is required to investigate the origin of the British flapjack and, sadly, this falls outside the scope of this book.

Where to next?

In Australia and New Zealand many of the popular baking recipes found their way into published cookery books, as well as handwritten family recipe books and newspapers. It was in an Australian newspaper publication that I discovered the first recipe using the word 'ANZAC'. The next chapter will look at the first time the ANZAC acronym was used in Australia and New Zealand to describe a food, and in particular this iconic biscuit. This chapter will also consider similar Anzac biscuit recipes published between 1916 and 1940 – only to find that they went by a multitude of different names. Nothing is simple!

Chapter 3
What's in a Name?

The first use of the word 'Anzac' in baking recipes

Before discussing the first use of the word Anzac in baking terms, we need to understand its background and meaning. The Australian Government's Department of Veterans' Affairs states:

> Historically, ANZAC (Australian and New Zealand Army Corps) was an acronym devised by Major General William Birdwood's staff in Cairo in early 1915. It was used for registering correspondence for the new corps. After the landing at Gallipoli, General Birdwood requested that the position held by the Australians and New Zealanders on the peninsula be called 'Anzac' to distinguish it from the British position at Helles. Not surprisingly, the word was soon applied to the men of the corps who became 'Anzacs'.

After the horrors of Gallipoli, many of the surviving Anzac forces were deployed to France where they went on to fight in bloody battles on the Western Front. By the end of the First World War in 1919, the returning military forces were proudly welcomed home with Anzac parades, Anzac parties, Anzac picnics, Anzac buffets and other Anzac social events. As a continuing mark of respect, and as a way of honouring the brave Gallipoli diggers, buildings, streets and highways were given the name Anzac. This use of the acronym ANZAC also applied to some food items.

During the Great War years the names of some of the popular baking recipes changed, in particular homemade cakes and biscuits. Biscuits baked by the women at home represented a significant contribution to the war effort. The act of baking biscuits was a positive, emotional and economical way for women to honour their brave diggers. This everyday form of food preparation gave them a physical connection, bringing them closer to their loved ones overseas. These homemade cakes and biscuits were packed and included in 'comforts parcels' and posted overseas, or sold at local patriotic fundraising events.

Despite extensive research I have not been able to identify exactly when the biscuit name changed, but I have found evidence that not long after the Gallipoli campaign of 1915 biscuit names and other foods such as cakes and puddings were changed to include the word Anzac or Gallipoli, or replaced with other patriotic names.

In some cases, the change came surprisingly quickly. Nowhere is this more apparent than in the 1916 1st edition *PWMU Cookery Book of Victoria*, compiled and issued by the Presbyterian Women's Missionary Union of Victoria.

Among the 'Scones and Teacakes' recipes there is 'Gallipoli Tea Cakes', a simple plain sponge cake with a cinnamon crumble topping. This sweet and spicy crumbly mixture was similar to the continental streusel topping found in early Australian cookery books and family recipe notebooks under recipes for 'coffee cake', a cake to serve with coffee, not coffee-flavoured!

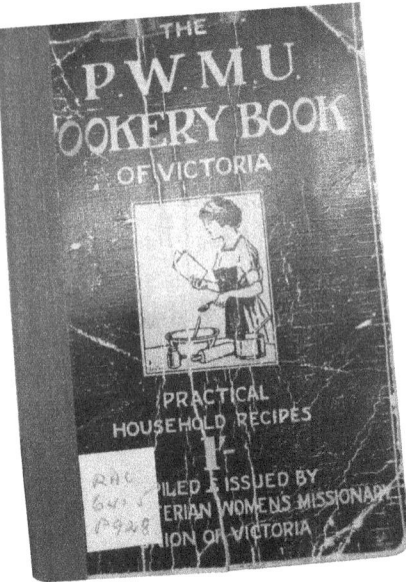

Cover of the *PWMU Cookery Book of Victoria: Practical Household Recipes*, compiled by the Presbyterian Women's Missionary Union of Victoria, 1916, and the Gallipoli Tea Cakes recipe found inside.

A slice of Gallipoli tea cake.
(Photographer Nicki Agars, 2013)

Common ingredients and method of making

Pre-1915, biscuit recipes similar to the Anzac biscuit went by different names, such as rolled oat biscuits, oatmeal biscuits, quick biscuits and surprise biscuits. They share the common ingredients – rolled oats, flour, sugar, butter and bicarbonate of soda – but none of them contain golden syrup or coconut. In Chapter 7 I delve more deeply into the question of who put the coconut in the Anzac biscuit. These speedy biscuits were made by the 'melting method', the same quick method that is used to make Anzac biscuits today. The early biscuits were also finished in the same way as today's Anzac biscuits.

What's in a Name?

Later, the renaming of some of these biscuits as soldiers' biscuits, Red Cross biscuits and eventually Anzac biscuits, helped to enhance the many fundraising efforts that continued throughout the war on the home front. More importantly, the Anzac biscuit went on to create a connection with the diggers that has remained a lasting legacy in Australia and New Zealand.

Newspapers of the day were a wonderful source of new and popular recipes and could be promptly shared among friends.

The earliest Australian Anzac biscuit recipe published in a newspaper

Mrs M. Sutherland submitted and won fourth prize for her recipe, Anzac Ginger Biscuits, published in a Perth newspaper, the *Sunday Times*, 4 June 1916. The recipe combined treacle, dripping or butter, sugar and milk, which was then heated. The melted mixture was then added to ginger, baking soda 'and enough flour to roll out stiff, cut round and bake in a moderate

Fourth Prize

Fourth prize is awarded to Mrs. M. Sutherland, Grosvenor, Mt. Kokeby, for recipe—

ANZAC GINGER BISCUITS.

Ingredients: One cup treacle, quarter-cup dripping or butter, quarter-cup sugar, quarter-cup milk. Put on stove to make hot. Then put in dessertspoonful of ginger, one teaspoonful of baking soda and enough flour to roll out stiff. Cut round. Bake in moderate oven.

Fourth prize for Anzac Ginger Biscuits recipe, published in the *Sunday Times* (Perth), 4 June 1916.

oven'. As with Anzacs, there are no eggs, and the ingredients are combined using the melting method. However, the recipe does not contain oats and the finish is different. On the other hand, this recipe does demonstrate the connection to ginger biscuits explored in Chapter 2.

Interestingly, on 10 August 1918, the Adelaide newspaper the *Mail* published a recipe for rolled oat biscuits. This biscuit has the same ingredients (including golden syrup), the same melting method, and the same finishing technique as Anzac biscuits – but it had another name!

Newspapers regularly requested and printed recipes for their readers. The 'Kitchen and Pantry' section of the Melbourne *Argus*, 15 September 1920, published a recipe for Anzac biscuits or crispies. The recipe had been kindly submitted by 'Josephine' of East Brunswick and listed 'two cups of John Bull Oats or flakes, not meal' in the list of ingredients. The last two lines of the recipe are interesting: 'They must be very ripe when ready for the table. They are usually eaten with a spoon.' A printing mistake I think!

ANZAC BISCUITS OR CRISPIES.
"Josephine" (E. Brunswick) has been kind enough to contribute the following recipe for Anzac biscuits:—Two cups John Bull oats or flaked oat meal, 1 cup flour, 1 table-spoonful golden syrup, half-cup of sugar, 1 teaspoonful carbonate of soda, 1 good pinch salt, 2 tablespoonfuls boiling water, half-cup melted butter. Put oatmeal, flour, sugar, and salt together. Pour on the melted butter, mix syrup and boiling water, and stir in the soda. Mix all while frothing. Put on the greased oven slide with a teaspoon, bake brown, in a moderate oven. They must be very ripe when ready for the table. They are usually eaten with a spoon.

Josephine's recipe for Anzac Biscuits or Crispies,
published in the *Argus* (Melbourne), 15 September 1920.

What's in a Name?

Within a year (22 June 1921), the *Argus* published a request for a biscuit recipe from 'Jeanette' of Yarrawonga for 'John Bull or Anzac biscuits, made with John Bull oats, and including treacle ...'

The John Bull oats company may well have published a recipe on their packets of oats but I have not found evidence of this. However, as well as newspaper recipes I have seen several family recipe notebooks specifying John Bull oats in their Anzac biscuit recipe.

While popular recipes of the day are printed in newspapers fairly quickly, it can take much longer, sometimes several years, for new recipes to be published in cookery books.

The earliest Anzac biscuit recipe published in an Australian cookery book

The *War Chest Cookery Book*, published in 1917 by the Sydney War Chest Fund, contains the earliest reference in an Australian cookery book to Anzac biscuits. Once again, this Anzac biscuit recipe is very different to the one we use today. The ingredients include sugar, butter, eggs, flour, rice flour, baking powder, cinnamon and spice; there are no oats, golden syrup or coconut. This recipe is made by the creaming method and the dough is rolled out, cut and baked. When cold the biscuits are sandwiched together with jam and iced – a very different Anzac biscuit.

The next recipe on the page, just called 'Biscuits', was contributed by Mary Ralston of the War Chest Depot. These are made by melting butter and adding boiling water; this wet mixture is then added to the dry ingredients – flour, brown sugar, rolled oats and soda – but is still missing the golden syrup. Again, the finish is different; the dough is rolled out and then cut into fancy shapes.

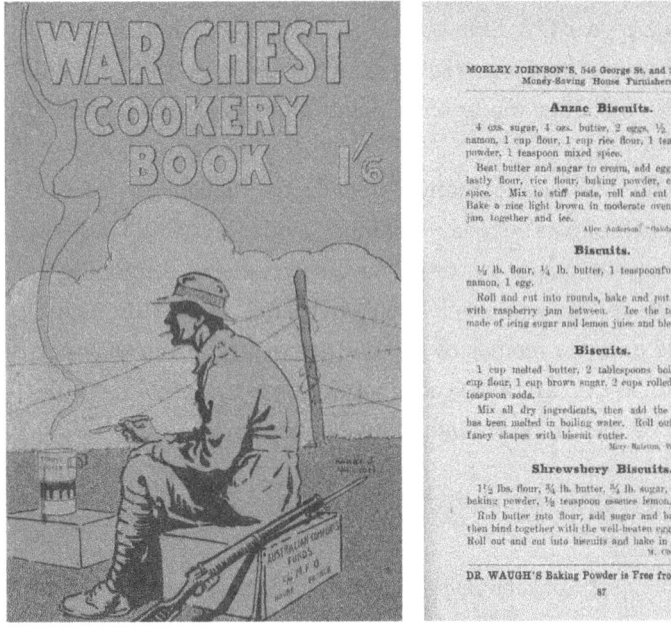

Cover of the *War Chest Cookery Book*, 1917,
and the recipes for Anzac Biscuits and for Biscuits.
(National Library of Australia)

Further on in the same book (page 91) is the Rolled Oat Biscuits recipe, which includes rolled oats, salt, flour and brown sugar; these are mixed with butter 'melted to a liquid' and finally 'carbonate of soda' dissolved in boiling water. Again, no golden syrup but this time, small pieces are taken from the mixture, rolled into balls between the hands and flattened out before being baked. Both the 'Biscuits' recipe and the Rolled Oat Biscuits are without spices. By the inclusion of most of the same ingredients, the same method of making and the same finishing technique we are now getting much closer to the Anzac biscuit we know today.

> **Rolled Oats Biscuits.**
>
> Mix 2 cups rolled oats, pinch salt, 1 cup flour, 1 cup brown sugar.
>
> Rub all well together with hands, then add ½ cup butter (melted to a liquid) and, last of all, ½ teaspoon carbonate soda dissolved in about 2 tablespoons boiling water; let stand for ten minutes, then take a small piece and roll in balls between hands and flatten out. Bake on a buttered slide in a fairly hot oven.
>
> Mrs. R. Nosworthy, Corinda.

Rolled Oats Biscuits recipe from *War Chest Cookery Book*, 1917.

New Zealand and the Anzac name

While my research did not extend to investigating New Zealand newspaper recipes, family cookery notebooks or an extensive search of New Zealand's vintage cookery books, I have been in personal communication with Emeritus Professor Helen Leach, Anthropology Department, University of Otago.

Professor Leach first researched the Anzac biscuit for an address at the New Zealand Guild of Food Writers' Conference in 1999. Her research revealed an advertisement for Waitaki butter, which included a recipe for Anzac Cakes. It was found in the *St Andrew's Cookery Book* (7th edition) published in Dunedin in 1915. However, this recipe was more of a rock cake than a biscuit and did not include any mixing instructions.

Professor Leach also found a recipe for Anzac Pudding in the *Southland Red Cross Cookery Book* published in 1917 or 1918, and what we now know as an Anzac biscuit appeared under the name Rolled Oat Biscuits (as in the *Australian War Chest Cookery Book*, 1917).

According to Professor Leach there is a recipe for Anzac Crispies in the *St Andrew's Cookery Book* (8th edition) published

> One cup of flour, 1 cup ground rice, 1 cup sugar, ½ cup (small) of milk, 2oz of **Waitaki Butter,** 2 eggs, ½ packet mixed spice, 2 teaspoonfuls cream of tartar, 1 teaspoonful soda, a pinch of salt. Mix and roll out, cut into rounds, and when cooked stick two together with raspberry jam and ice.
>
> **Anzac Cakes.**
>
> Ingredients: One pound flour, ¼lb sugar, 6oz **Waitaki Butter,** 1 teaspoonful baking powder, ½lb fruit.

This advertisement for Waitaki butter included the Anzac Cakes recipe; from the 7th edition of the *St Andrew's Cookery Book*, published in Dunedin, 1915.

in 1919 and this appears to be the earliest published cookery book recipe with both the ingredients and the method that we now recognise as an Anzac biscuit (albeit without the coconut). The same recipe was also in subsequent editions.

Duncan Galletly, a member of the Food History Group of New Zealand and a cookery book collector checked his 5th, 6th, 7th, 8th and 9th editions of the *St Andrew's Cookery Book*. He was able to forward me the advertisement from the 7th and 8th editions for the Waitaki butter, which included the recipe for Anzac Cakes. In 2012, the Methodist paper *Touchstone* published an article by 'Yvonne'. The article, *A Fund Raising Experiment: Recipe for Success*, discusses the success of this fundraising community cookery book, the *St Andrew's Cookery Book,* from 1904 until the last edition in 1932. In fact, Yvonne goes as far as asserting 'that St Andrew's Dunedin women can claim the honour for the first published Anzac biscuit recipe'.

On the other hand, who is to say that the first recipe must be one that is published in a printed cookery book? As far as Australia is concerned there are several early newspaper recipes that carry the Anzac name, and I'm sure the same would apply in New Zealand. Similarly, where do the heirloom family recipes

What's in a Name?

Foreword and Anzac Crispies recipe published in the 8th edition of the St Andrew's Cookery Book, 1919.

fit in? Their existence indicates that the Anzac biscuit recipe would have been in circulation well before it was published in a cookery book.

I believe these recipes were all appearing at about the same time and evolved simultaneously. As far as Australia and New Zealand are concerned, Professor Leach acknowledged that people on both sides of the Tasman were following parallel paths when it came to renaming different items in commemoration of the Anzac forces. As for the Anzac biscuit, it's only natural that something so successful would be shared in every form of communication available at the time.

This Anzac biscuit journey has only just begun!

Chapter 4

Jaw Breakers
The Anzac wafer or tile

Hard biscuits for hard times

The Anzac biscuit discussed in previous chapters is the sweet biscuit made from rolled oats and golden syrup, the homemade biscuit that we now know went by many different names! To confuse us further, there is another biscuit that changed its name during WWI. This was the army biscuit, a commercially produced hardtack biscuit integral to army 'iron' (emergency) rations. These iron rations were issued to military forces well before WWI, for example Australian soldiers fighting in the Anglo–Boer War (1899–1902) were issued hardtack biscuits.

British author Sue Shephard in *Pickled, Potted & Canned: How the Art and Science of Food Preserving Changed the World* writes that 'throughout history, hard biscuits have been the mainstay of armed forces on land and at sea'. In her first chapter Shephard discusses 'Drying' and devotes five pages to explaining the history of hardtack:

> Hardtack – also known as 'ship's biscuit' or 'pilot bread' – was the staple provision for anyone who set out on a long and perilous journey, be they sailor, soldier, traveller, explorer or migrant.

Shephard continues:

> The essential point of these biscuits is that they contain neither fats nor moisture and therefore keep for a long time. Traditionally, they were made from a dough of flour and water, baked and dried to a state of 'immortal' hardness.

Unlike bread, hardtack biscuits did not go mouldy. Made from flour, salt and water and baked until they were rock hard, these biscuits were used as a bread substitute. By the end of the 19th century 'factories equipped with modern machinery turn them out in tons' writes baker turned author, Frederick T. Vine.

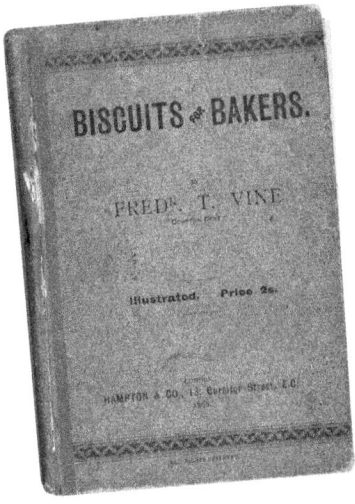 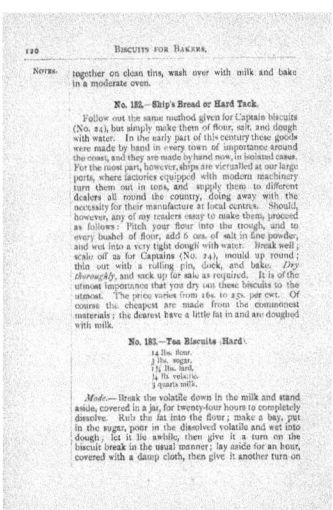

No. 182–Ship's Bread or Hard Tack recipe found in *Biscuits for Bakers* by Frederick T. Vine , published in London, 1896.

Originally, the hardtack biscuits, also called 'navy' or 'ship's' biscuits, were smaller than the army biscuit. Army biscuits packed and stored well. This was an important consideration in the early months at Gallipoli where it was not always possible to maintain supplies of fresh food.

An article in the *Yea Chronicle* reveals how the soldiers' war-biscuit was an important part of wartime food during the siege of Paris by the German army in the Franco–Prussian War of 1870. The newspaper describes how a London firm of biscuit makers received an urgent order (that came out of Paris by balloon) for 're-victualling of the city' with 60 million ship's or navy biscuits.

Why did the name change from army biscuits to Anzac biscuits during World War I? An understanding of the conditions that the Australian and New Zealand soldiers experienced at Gallipoli, as well as their courage and bravery in battle, may provide us with some of the answers.

Harsh conditions at Gallipoli

Weather conditions were often extreme at Gallipoli. There was relentless heat in the summer (which brought with it endless flies and related illnesses); bitter cold, frosts and snow in winter as well as torrential rainstorms which constantly flooded the trenches. These harsh conditions exacerbated the many challenges the army faced in feeding the soldiers. Fresh food and water were scarce. Sometimes fresh bread, bacon and cheese came through, but most of the time the food varied little and it consisted mainly of bully beef (canned beef), hard biscuits (army biscuits), tea, sugar and jam. Soldiers drank lots of tea, which had to come out of their water ration of 2.3 litres per day. So precious was the water that any leftover tea was used for shaving!

The *Discovering Gallipoli Research Guide* defines the hardtack biscuit supplied to the AIF (Australian Imperial Force – on overseas service) in place of bread as 'one of the most durable materials used in the war, reputed to be bullet proof!'.

Many soldiers' letters confirm that hardtack biscuits were indeed unpalatable and because of this they became notorious. It was as a result of the army biscuit's constant use during the early stages of the Gallipoli campaign that they became known as the Anzac wafer or tile. Ironically, and in keeping with the diggers' sense of humour, these biscuits were anything but the thin, light and crispy 'wafer' their name suggests. In reality, these army biscuits were so hard that soldiers nicknamed them 'jaw breakers' or 'dog biscuits'. Their oblong shape and weight may well have contributed to them also being referred to as Anzac tiles.

Paul Teesdale Smith (2nd AIF, 9th Light Horse Regiment) mentions army biscuits several times in his letters home. He describes dreaming of 'something nice to eat', the monotony of army biscuits and, to his surprise, how the 'iron rations' were embraced by local villagers:

> Gallipoli (undated). I'm beginning to dream of something nice to eat. Your scrambled eggs wouldn't go badly but I see large rounds of undercut steak with poached eggs on top. Fresh, thick-sliced brown bread, new butter and bottles of beer. They revolve slowly around me but so far I have never been able to stop one. Whenever I make a grab they turn into bully beef tins, biscuits and a water bottle.

Anzac Biscuits

3 November 1915 So long, I'm just going after the rations. There's bread and frozen meat today. You don't realise how nice bread is till you've lived on biscuits for a while.

12 December 1916 In the afternoon lots of the villagers came round the camps (for) bucksheesh [see definition in glossary] bully and biscuits. First people I've seen eat b & b with any show of enjoyment.

Food – something to write home about

There was little that the troops could write home about because of military mail censorship. However, they could describe the food they were eating, and letters from soldiers reveal how resourceful they were when it came to 'having a good feed'. Some were luckier than others. Writing from Anzac Cove, 22 July 1915, Norman Bethune (8th Light Horse Regiment) describes how soldiers took advantage of local produce to supplement the army rations:

> It has been a bit of a change coming back to bully beef and biscuits again, but we really are well fed and get as well cheese, bacon, bread (the latter about every other day) tea, jam, sugar and occasionally rice. The last mentioned is good as a pudding of course, or can be made into quite appetizing dishes when mixed with beef. Thyme grows about here wild which is very handy.

Oranges and radishes were also purchased from local people by Lieutenant J.R.B. Love (14th Light Horse Regiment) while he was serving in Egypt. Love frequently wrote home to his family in Strathalbyn, South Australia, thanking them for the many parcels and letters he received and describing the food on the troop ships as good and the bread excellent. However, it was a different story on land when the army food was down to bare rations of bully beef and hard biscuits, jam and tea.

Love writes that 'the everlasting marmalade was always good'. On another occasion he wrote: 'While camped on the Canal we caught plenty of fish.' This was just as well as he was not so keen on the quality of the bully beef. In his opinion 'the New Zealand bully beef was much better than the very poor American stuff we usually get'.

It appears that the Australian meat canning industry was unable to meet all the Australian army's requirements. In a later letter Love tells his family that when they entered the abandoned Turkish army headquarters they found 400,000 tins of German bully beef, which was even worse!

Diggers' letters published in the local newspaper

In Australia it was common for soldiers' letters to be published in local newspapers and the monotony of 'iron rations' was a constant point of discussion. The Anzac wafer or tile featured in a long letter published in the *Queanbeyan Age* in February 1916. Writing to his mother Mrs J.H. Fitzgibbons from Heliopolis on 26 December 1915, Private Erle Capes (AMC) describes the hardship and abundance:

Members of the 4th Australian Field Ambulance on Lemnos, December 1915, displaying the contents of their Christmas billies, which all included a pipe and food. They are wearing the lids on their heads. (AWM P001116.024)

I suppose you know we have left the Peninsula and I am not sorry either. It was getting very cold and we had heavy snow. Was on short allowance befo'e we left Anzac – three biscuits per day per man and one tin of jam among six of us. I tell you I was glad to see Egypt again; it was like home.

Capes continues by describing his Christmas:

> We had a splendid Christmas dinner – turkey, ham and everything you could mention. Our officers got one of the restaurants to cater for us at our own camp. Had great fun with the billy can. Got one each with all sorts of things in them quite a nice little present.

Christmas in the trenches

Soldiers' Christmas experiences varied considerably, and sometimes they were memorable for all the wrong reasons.

Corporal R. Brown (5th ALTM Battery 2nd Division AIF) writes thanking the people of Orange for all their Christmas greetings. The letter was published on page one of the *Leader* (Orange, NSW) on 30 January 1918. The column title is *ORANGE SOLDIERS' XMAS GIFTS,* the subtitle: *THE FIRST ACKNOWLEDGMENT.*

> Still Here 'Somewhere', 20/11/17:
> To the people of Orange per favor of Mrs E.T. McNeilly and Mrs Homley: Will you please convey to the residents of Orange my sincere thanks for the lovely message of greetings that I received today. I am sure every one of we boys on this side of the globe appreciate the kind thoughts of the people at home.

Later his letter included a vivid description of a 'memorable' Christmas the year before:

> It is hard times having to be in the trenches for Xmas (we were there last Xmas), I will never forget our last Xmas. We went into the trenches three days before the festival, and all

we could get to eat was 'bully' and 'Anzac wafers' (army No. 10 biscuits). Xmas day we had nothing, as our ration party was skittled by Fritz on their way up to the trenches.

Brown concludes his letter with 'PS If anyone would like to correspond I would be thankful. Failing that send the Orange "Leader"'.

Desperate times call for desperate measures

A chapter is devoted to 'The Army Biscuit' in *The ANZAC Book: written and illustrated in Gallipoli by the men of ANZAC* and published in 1916. O.E. Burton NZMC discusses whether hardtack biscuits are a blessing or a curse and the part they play in the soldiers' daily routine – 'the carrying of them, the eating of them, the cursing at them!'. He stresses how hard the biscuits were and how they sometimes broke teeth, and outlines the numerous ways in which the biscuits are made edible: 'We pound them to powder. We boil them with bully. We stew them in stews. We fry them as fritters.' Burton also analyses the taste and concludes, 'Army biscuits taste like nothing else on the Gallipoli Peninsula'. As the biscuits were such a significant part of army existence he admits to an attachment with a degree of humour:

> Biscuits! Army biscuits. They are old friends now, and, like all old friends, they will stand much hard wear and tear. Well glazed, they would make excellent tiles or fine flagstones.

Making the hardtack biscuits edible was a constant challenge for the troops. Ever resourceful, someone created a grater from a piece of metal so the biscuits could be reduced to small

Jaw Breakers

Images from the *ANZAC Book*.
'A Present From Home' by David Barker, Gallipoli, 1915. This cartoon shows a soldier receiving a cookery book with just a tin of Fray Bentos bully beef and army biscuits etc. The caption reads: 'Do they think we're on a bloomin' pic-nic?' 'Each One Doing His Bit' is drawn by Otho Hewett, Gallipoli, 1915. It illustrates the different rations: bully beef, army biscuit, apricot jam, matches, rum, milk etc. all worn by soldiers in khaki, except for the army biscuit which is worn by a knight in shining armour illustrating the toughness of the biscuit!

shreds and then softened in water and turned into a form of porridge. In a letter written from the trenches, South Australian Barossa Valley watchmaker Private Victor Offe (Machine Gun Company, 32 Battalion) includes a recipe for 'Trench Porridge'.

> **A SOLDIER'S RECIPE FROM FRANCE—HOW TO MAKE "TRENCH PORRIDGE."**
>
> Take ½ lb. Anzac wafers, commonly known as whole meal biscuits or jaw breakers, powder up, and soak overnight in about 1 pint of water—shellhole water if procurable. Care must be taken in the soaking stage, or the biscuits may get too soft (I don't think). Next day boi for about 20 minutes, than add quarter lb. raisins, and boil for another 10 minutes. Then add milk and sugar to taste. If prepared in this way a most nourishing and tasty dish will be the result.
>
> Sent by PTE. VICTOR OFFE, Machine Gun Company.

Coincidentally, the letter arrived around the same time the local *Barossa News* issued a request for recipes to be included in a *Barossa Cookery Book*. The paper declared 'All proceeds other than bare expenses go to SA Soldiers' Fund'. Private Offe's sister handed over the Trench Porridge recipe to the committee and it was one of the *400 Tried Recipes* chosen for the 1st edition *Barossa Cookery Book* (*BCB*) in 1917 (see page 54 for more information on the *BCB*). A printing mistake (corrected for the 2nd edition, December 1922) shows the last few lines of the recipe were printed upside down. I don't think this error would have concerned Private Offe as his recipe denotes a good sense of humour. Other Offe family recipes were included in the 1st edition.

Anzac wafers or tiles – not just for eating!

Soldiers creatively made use of hardtack biscuits as a way of solving the shortage of stationery. They wrote messages on them, painted pictures on them, and even used them as photo frames in order to have something to post overseas to their loved ones at Christmas.

Title page of the *Barossa Cookery Book: Four Hundred Tried Recipes*, published in Tanunda, South Australia, in 1917, and the Trench Porridge recipe found inside (with the last line upside down in the 1st edition of 1917, but corrected for the 2nd edition in 1922).

Finding Private Offe

After all this research on the Trench Porridge recipe my colleagues and I felt rather attached to Private Offe. Thanks to the help of David Farlan, a military history expert, we were relieved to discover that Private Offe did eventually return home (albeit with trench fever) in 1917. Family history researcher Judith Lydeamore managed to track down Private Offe's granddaughter, Victoria Petho. It was reassuring to find that the descendants of Private Offe still have and treasure his valuable correspondence.

Private Christmas's army biscuit.
(AWM REL/00918)

The appropriately named Private C.R. Christmas, (5 Field Ambulance, AIF) used an army biscuit as a Christmas card from Gallipoli in 1915. This exhibit is held in the Heraldry collection of the Australian War Museum (AWM) in Canberra. The AWM describe the damaged biscuit as having one remaining complete edge, which says 'OLD FRIENDS ANZAC' in black ink, and can be seen in the photo above. The message on the back of the biscuit, some of which is illegible, reads: 'Merry Christmas Prosperous New Year from Old friends ANZAC Gallipoli 1915 Private C.R. Christmas MM 3903 AIF AAMC'.

In writing about 'Trench Culture of the Great War' for the publication *Folklore*, Graham Seal describes the many trench names used for army food by the British Tommy. Seal naturally includes the army biscuit:

> A 'wad' was a sandwich, while 'hard tack' was the traditional dry biscuit, or iron rations, of the British soldier. Usually

eaten with 'bully' beef, or tinned beef, these items were also said to be useful for lighting fires.

War memorabilia becomes collectors' treasures

Two individual army biscuits, kept as souvenirs from the frontline by Lt Lionel Bruce Charles of the 5th Battalion, The Queen's Regiment, were sold in an auction on 18–19 June 2014 to a London dealer for £290. This unusual find was revealed in the article 'Taking The Biscuit' from *The Art Market Weekly, Antiques Trade Gazette*. The journal says:

> one of the most unusual lots must surely be these biscuits offered by Lockdales of Ipswich ... Their labels read 'Biscuits used by troops in Suvla Bay', one marked for Gallipoli and the other for Dardanelles, August 1915.

Clearly these 'jaw breakers' survived dunkin' and a century later have withstood the test of time!

When did the name change?

Piled up high, waiting on the side of the wharf to be shipped to the troops, were boxes and boxes of army biscuits. Before these cartons were loaded, wharfies would scribble the acronym ANZAC across the outside; this was the way in which the army ensured that the diggers' packing cases reached the rightful destination. I wonder if this action contributed to the name change from army biscuit to Anzac wafer or tile? Alternatively, was the army biscuit renamed after Gallipoli because these hardtack biscuits were so notorious there? Or, was this a way of acknowledging the spirit and bravery of the Anzac fighting forces.

The Barossa Cookery Book

The 1st edition of *The Barossa Cookery Book* was supported by local advertisements, but it did not have an index, contents page or page numbers. The recipes were listed under different sections (see below) and the book asserts that these recipes 'bear the signature of each donor as a guarantee of faith'. Price sixpence.

Sections in *The Barossa Cookery Book*:

Soup: 4 recipes, including 3 tomato soups

Entrée: 20 recipes, including Cold Pigeon Pie submitted by Mrs Eddy Offe, Tanunda. (Could she be a relative?)

Pudding: 49 recipes, including War Time Plum Pudding made with mashed carrot and potatoes. Private Victor Offe's recipe for Trench Porridge appears here.

Biscuits: 27 recipes with a wide variety of ingredients including oatmeal, rolled oats, ginger, cinnamon, cocoanut, lemons, almonds and dates – but surprisingly no recipe that resembles today's Anzac biscuit.

Cake: 116 recipes, tagged on at the end of the biscuit recipes. By the second edition (1922) cakes have their own section. Mrs H. Offe, Tanunda (could this be Hannah Offe, Private Offe's mother?) submitted one of two sultana cake recipes. There are also three recipes for the fashionable Lamington Cake (lamingtons).

Scones and Rolls: 6 recipes, in their own section

Jellies, Jams and Preserves: 46 recipes also in their own section.

At the back of the book, the sections are divided into Drinks (3 recipes), Sweets (9 recipes) and finally a miscellaneous recipe section: Fruit Salts, Preserved Butter and Home-made Soap.

Chapter 5
Something from Home

The female instinct – nurturing and patriotic
At the beginning of the Great War women at home were worried that their loved ones on the frontline were under-nourished. They wanted to ensure that what was sent in care packages from home would add to the troops' nutritional needs. Homemade cakes and biscuits were ideal foods to give them much needed energy and a treat, and break the monotony of army rations.

Although there is proof that fruit cakes and plum puddings (at Christmas) were sent overseas, it has been hard to find evidence that the same applied to home-baked biscuits and, in particular, the Anzac biscuit. Two leading food historians suggest that this is one of the myths surrounding the Anzac biscuit. In 1999, Emeritus Professor Helen Leach from New Zealand wrote:

> I have seen no documentary evidence that any items called Anzac Biscuits/Crispies or Rolled Oat Biscuits/Crispies were included in the soldiers' comfort parcels sent to troops in WW1. In view of the interest in soldiers' diaries from the Gallipoli campaign and the later campaign on the Western Front any mention of Anzac Biscuits would surely have been noted by now. That items called Anzac Biscuits were actually sent to New Zealand or Australian troops in the period 1915–1918 remains a myth. To my mind, all the food items named after the Anzac troops were purely commemorative.

This thinking has been shared by Australia's eminent food historian Barbara Santich, who writes that this is a sentimental story that blends 'female nurturing instinct with patriotic duty', it is 'in the popular imagination' and 'it is what we would all like to believe'. Santich continues: 'There is no evidence that Australian women packed tins of homemade biscuits and dispatched them off to loved ones in the trenches.'

On the other hand, in writing about women on the home front in *Anzac Biscuits: A Culinary Memorial*, Australian academic Dr Sian Supski suggests that it seems likely that a biscuit resembling an Anzac biscuit would have been sent to soldiers. Supski reinforces this assumption by referring to The Australian Comforts Fund (Victorian Division) list that requests biscuits and cakes to be packed in sealed tins.

Lois Daish of the New Zealand *Listener* regularly updated her Anzac biscuit history information to share with her readers. In July 1994 she wrote:

> At first I despaired of there being any truth to the myth that I grew up with, that these biscuits were sent in food parcels to soldiers in the trenches of Europe. Then I received a phone call from Beverley Bennett, who told me that her mother, Edith Shore, now aged 92, has clear memories of her girlhood during World War I, when she had helped her own mother pack Anzac biscuits into large golden syrup tins, which were then sent off to the front. The sending of food parcels to troops overseas, a common activity in World War II was apparently unusual in World War I: except for small items, such as tinned lollies and sardines.

Around the same time there were urgent appeals in newspapers for tins needed to dispatch biscuits, supporting Dr Supski's argument:

> *Ovens and Murray* Advertiser, *Beechworth, Victoria, 15 June 1918*
>
> Beechworth Red Cross Society 1918 urgent appeal for petrol, benzine and kerosene tins in which to dispatch biscuits to our prisoners of war. 6000 of these tins are needed a month ... 7lb treacle and golden syrup tins ... as it is in these the sweets our boys long for are sent. Please help with a full supply of tins so that our unfor-unate (sic) heroes may receive these comforts.

7 lb. golden syrup tins. (Beth Farlam collection)

To date I have not had access to soldiers' diaries but a chance conversation with a friend gave me my first opportunity to read some treasured diggers' letters. I wondered if these letters would at last confirm what we would all like to believe. Would there be a mention of receiving homemade biscuits? Over time, as more letters and diaries come to light, I am hopeful other references to receiving biscuits will be uncovered.

Comforts and mail – good for morale

Soldiers' letters mention biscuits among the food received in parcels from home. However, identifying whether these were homemade biscuits is not so easy. Were these biscuits the precursor to the Anzac biscuit? Were they the soldiers' biscuit, or the Red Cross biscuit, or biscuits known by the other names used prior to or during the war years?

Back on the home front, women were doing their bit to support the war effort and were always looking for ways to raise money for the various patriotic war funds. Home-baked biscuits were an affordable contribution to sell and to serve with light refreshments at any fundraising event. Giving names to the biscuits that 'linked with the war' was a way in which ordinary women could connect. This was their contribution to a bigger cause. Once it was established that these biscuits suited all the requirements for posting overseas, the meaning and association grew. Exactly when the different biscuit names were changed and when they all became known as Anzac biscuits is, of course, the million-dollar question.

Letters written by soldiers to those at home stressed the importance of receiving mail and packages. Great examples are the letters of the Bethune Brothers from Victoria.

Brothers Alexander Douglas ('Doug') Bethune and Norman McLeod Bethune both served with the 8th Light Horse Regiment. Douglas was a Corporal in B Squadron AIF and was killed in action on 7 August 1915 at the infamous Battle of the Nek, Gallipoli. Norman was a trooper killed in action on 19 April 1917 at Aseifiyeh, Palestine. Letters to their sister Dolly in Melbourne were descriptive, as far as they were allowed to be, and they did their best to sound cheerful so as to not cause too much distress. Dolly wrote back regularly to both of them, and sent parcels, she knew just how much it would lift their spirits. The importance of mail day was often stressed in Doug's letters. Letter to 'Dear old Doll' from Mena Camp Egypt:

> Mail Day is the greatest institution we have, and is more important than pay day. AD Bethune 15.4.15

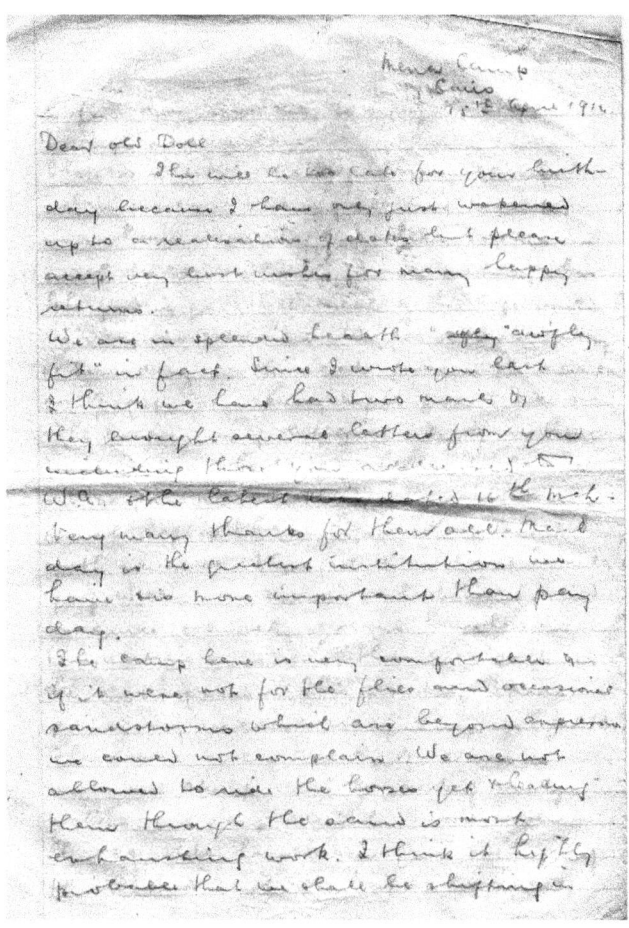

Mail day. Post is being distributed to men of the 1st Australian Light Horse Field Ambulance, Chailak Dere, on the Gallipoli Peninsula, Turkey, 1915. (AWM C03613)

A group of Australian soldiers at an open-air cookhouse, Mena Camp, Egypt, 1915. (OM65-30/14, Box 8579, State Library of Queensland)

And a few months later from the desert:

> Very many thanks for being so good about writing, I live for mail days. ADB 20.07.15

Eighteen months later, brother Norman Bethune is stationed in the desert and writes to Dolly about his latest parcel:

> From the Desert
>
> Dearest Dolly,
> Your parcel with the Bulletins, cheese and biscuits arrived safely. The cheese I am keeping for our next trip out, if we have one, . . . and the biscuits were delicious. I wonder did you make them yourself.
> NM Bethune 14.1.17

There was always a shortage of news for the troops so the *Bulletin* (an Australian magazine) was welcome reading material. The cheese would have come in a tin and Norman would have enjoyed keeping this little luxury to liven up one of his overnight expeditions into the desert. Obviously the biscuits, being delicious, were eaten immediately and the fact that he asks Dolly, 'I wonder did you make them yourself?' confirms that Norman identified these as homemade biscuits. Unfortunately, we don't know what Dolly replied. By 1917, many of the army camps provided canteens where soldiers could purchase packets of commercial biscuits and these homemade biscuits would not only have looked different, they would have tasted different too.

As letters were censored by the military, soldiers could not write about where they were or what they were doing. As is often the case when away from home, food figures highly and naturally there were many references to the monotony of the army rations of 'bully beef and biscuits'.

Paul Teesdale Smith from South Australia

Biscuits warranted a mention in two letters home by a young digger Paul Teesdale Smith (2nd AIF 9th Light Horse Regiment 3rd Light Horse Brigade B Squadron A Troop) to his girlfriend Helen living in the Adelaide Hills. The biscuits were made by Joyce (Helen's sister) and in a later letter there is another mention of receiving biscuits as well as De Reszke and Three Castles cigarettes.

In letters to his soon-to-be wife, Paul Teesdale Smith writes:

> Gallipoli (undated)
>
> Supper commenced by killing a six inch centipede and eating some of Joyce's biscuits, very tasty, with chicken and ham paste, raspberry jam followed by an unlimited quantity and we drank 'Hell to the Kaiser' in a flowing bowl of cocoa.

> Gallipoli (undated)
>
> Nothing doing in the warline this week, but a great lot of parcels. Raisins, Peanuts, Biscuits, De Reszke, Three Castles, and socks and butterscotch I'm eating on now. It's wonderful how little things, no matter what they are, break the monotony.

We know that mail and parcels were popular and good for troop morale but sometimes the sheer number of them and the condition of the packages created problems and this took time and expertise to resolve.

Inappropriate packaging often led to parcels arriving damaged and folks at home gave little consideration to the different seasons being experienced by the troops. Sometimes inappropriate food was included and poorly packed liquids would break and ruin other parcels, causing wastage. Smells were a problem too – not just food that had gone off. This might in turn cause whole cases of packages to be destroyed; many a digger's prized Australian tobacco was unusable due to being packed too closely to a bar of soap!

In another example, Paul Teesdale Smith was unfortunate enough to be on the receiving end of bad eggs! His letter also confirms that canteens were well established in camps by 1917 but despite this he finishes his letter with a request for home-baked goods:

> 5 Dec 1917 The eggs arrived but the cigars haven't yet. The eggs I'm afraid were a failure, all the ones that had cracked were distinctly bad, the one that hadn't was, well you know it was, Um! Doubtful. Cakes all go down the same way. Tucker isn't the proposition it used to be, we've got canteens always on the spot nowadays, and our issue and canteen stores keep us going usually. Scrambled eggs for breakfast, toast and coffee. Cold meat, spuds, bread and butter for lunch. Baked meat and vegetables for tea. Frills like kidneys, sausages, fish thrown in to vary the diet. Everything except the issue is canned. Cakes, biscuits, shortbread are always appreciated. A few sweets too. PTS

Crumbs!

Delivering care packages to troops overseas was not a simple affair. Just dealing with the number of private parcels was a logistical nightmare for the postal services. Many cases of 'private parcels' were held up on wharves and waited weeks for space to be allocated on board merchant shipping, and that was before the two-month sea journey. There was extreme pressure for shipping space and the volume of postal parcels often exceeded the limited freight available. In June 1917, 250 tonnes a month was allocated. A special allotment of 800 extra tonnes needed for the troops' Christmas boxes in September was granted to a round of cheers from the Australian Comforts Fund committee.

Anzac nurses, serving in World War I, thoroughly appreciated receiving care packages from home. South Australian nurse Irene Bonnin wrote in her diary:

Had another parcel ... Anzac Nurse Irene Bonnin, diary entry 20 December 1915. (SLSA, PRG621_21_Parcel.)

20 Dec 1915 Had *another* parcel! ... each got a box like a large boot box tied up with R W & B ribbon given by the Australian womens league I believe in response to Lady Bridges appeal. Such jolly nice things – soap, scent, iodine and brush, boracic acid, stockings book, chocolates, biscuits, red cross brooch with 1915 on the back, block of postcards etc. Really such a very nice parcel. So awfully good of them to think of us.

The Australian Comforts Fund

The Australian Comforts Fund (ACF) was established in Sydney in 1916 in order to co-ordinate the state-based organisations (the various patriotic funds) set up mainly by women at the beginning of the war to provide and send comforts to soldiers in the battle zone. The ACF state bodies in World War I were:

New South Wales: Citizens' 'War Chest' Fund
Victoria: Lady Mayoress's Patriotic League
South Australia: League of Loyal Women
West Australia: Victoria League of West Australia
Queensland: Queensland Patriotic Fund
Tasmania: On Active Service Fund

The different divisions of the ACF were brought together to improve the distribution of packages and resolve some of the problems. The ACF provided a centralised administration that kept the divisions advised as to requirements and distribution. This also meant that the Department of Defence had only one Executive Head to deal with. The divisions bought and made items of food and clothing to send to the troops. The ACF also ran canteens near the frontlines that served food supplies and provided other items such as primus stoves, clothes, sporting

A pack transport column arriving at the 6th Battalion headquarters in the desert six miles from Seprapeum, Egypt, in February 1916. The horses are carrying gifts supplied by the Australian Comforts Fund.
(AWM C00203)

equipment, games, newspapers and magazines. The ACF ran a residential and recreational club for troops on leave in London called AIF and War Chest Club. The ACF ceased to operate on 10 April 1920.

Comfort parcels usually contained clothing, reading matter, tobacco, cigarettes and food. Hand-knitted hats, scarves, gloves and socks were much needed to combat the cold damp nights. However, half the parcels contained food and, as previously mentioned, a fruit cake was immensely popular; it kept well, usually arrived intact and therefore could be shared. In a letter to his 'Dearest Dolly' dated 8 December 1916, Norman Bethune confirms this:

Something from Home

The day your parcel arrived, I also got a parcel of good things from Chirita, and Auntie Molly's cake, which latter arrived in splendid condition and was just delicious. Myself and section (4 in a section as you know) enjoyed it very much, and others who were given a small piece were loud in praises. As usual, I cannot mention much of our doings or whereabouts.

A Christmas present for 'every Sailor afloat and every Soldier at the front' was the idea for an appeal by Princess Mary, the 17-year-old daughter of King George V and Queen Mary. These decorative brass tins were sent to members of the British, Colonial and Indian Armed forces for Christmas 1914.
(From the collection of Beth Farlam)

From fleece to sock ... Miss Coll is shown knitting socks direct from the fleece of a sheep in Melbourne, circa 1916. The Australian Comforts Fund then packed the socks into bales, as seen on the left of the photograph, and shipped them overseas to Australian troops.
(AWM H02438)

The homemade biscuit – a winner!

Fruit-cake ingredients were expensive, the cake was time-consuming to make and bake, as well as heavy and therefore costly to post. Luckily, there was no way that homemade Anzac-style biscuits would arrive as a pile of crumbs! They would have been packed in airtight tins so they could withstand the two- to three-month journey. Here was a nutritious snack from home that 'the boys' could enjoy and still share with their mates. For the women at home they were quick and easy to make from store

A parade of women and children aiding the Comforts Fund for
Australian Armed Forces Battalions in Brisbane, circa 1915.
(Negative 92287, record number 437891, State Library of Queensland)

cupboard ingredients and most important of all, affordable to send. The biscuit was a winner. Soldiers' letters I discovered have confirmed that homemade biscuits *were* sent to the troops in the period 1915–18 – so does this mean it is a myth no longer? Just when the biscuit name changed and became associated with the Anzac tradition has yet to be resolved.

Chapter 6

The Family Handwritten Recipe Book
A precious heirloom

To find historical evidence of Anzac biscuit recipes, a public call-to-arms was launched. As part of the 2011 South Australian history month I organised the first South Australian Cookbook Roadshow (SACRS). The aim was to source and examine pre-1940 Australian cookery books and in particular, hopefully, to see some family handwritten recipe books. The idea took off! Little did I realise how popular these SACRS gatherings would become; they have continued and I enjoy meeting the wonderful people who, like me, love sharing and talking about old cookery books.

The Cookbook Roadshow always involved a culinary presentation, such as 'Stir up Memories'. Community participation was much encouraged – attendees arrived at libraries, farmers' markets, schools and history centres with their treasured cookery book collections, including old published cookery books. Not surprisingly, the most treasured possessions were their heirloom recipe books.

Family handwritten recipe books provide us with an important source of information about the type of food available during a certain period of time, as well as the way in which food was prepared, cooked and served. Printed cookery books usually, but not always, include a publishing date; sadly, this is seldom the case for handwritten recipe books and a little bit of culinary detective work is essential to help date the recipes.

These notebooks are invariably battered and falling apart, with snippets of cooking hints scribbled alongside recipes. Over time, newspaper and magazine recipe cuttings are tucked in among the pages revealing household hints and the latest fashions. As these recipe books are handed down through the generations, the names on the inside front cover and the handwriting changes yet their precious value remains. One family recipe book in particular inspired me to research the origins, history, myths and legends surrounding the Anzac biscuit.

A little black recipe notebook

It was during a 2011 SA Cookbook Roadshow that I first met Carol Moore, from the Adelaide Hills, proudly presenting her grandmother's recipe notebook.

Carol's grandmother, Caroline Sarah Warner, started writing down her recipes when she married Gilbert Blythman in 1912. She first used it as a recipe book and then from 16 July 1915, ledger entries were added at the back for their farm sales of butter and eggs. The columns were costed in pounds, shillings and pence, and included the date of sales; this was a significant find. There were no entries in the ledger between 1917 and 1919.

Gilbert John Blythman enlisted in the AIF in June 1916 and then joined the 39th Battalion in France. Sadly, Gilbert's last postcard from France was sent in September 1917. It was not long after this that the sales of butter and eggs ceased to be recorded. The practice resumed two years later on 20 September 1919 and finished in March 1920 when the recipes from the front of the book met the ledger entries from the back. Most

Anzac Biscuits

handwritten recipe books do not give dates of entry, so having the ledger entries at the back with recorded dates is invaluable. The same handwriting continued throughout Caroline's recipe notebook.

Significantly, the third to last recipe in the book was for Anzac biscuits. This appears towards the end of the recipe section and we can therefore assume that this Anzac biscuit recipe was handwritten in either late 1919 or early 1920. This early recipe did not include coconut.

Pre-1920 Anzac Biscuit recipe from Caroline Warner's notebook, 1912–1920.

Strong patriotic feeling – recipes altered

Interestingly, there are recipes in Caroline Warner's notebook that reveal the strong patriotic feeling during the First World War; the titles of some pre-1914 recipes were later altered. For example 'German Coffee Cake' was crossed out with not one but two lines and replaced by 'Belgian Coffee Cake' (written in pencil). A few pages later there is a recipe for 'French Delight', which has exactly the same ingredients as the famous Turkish delight.

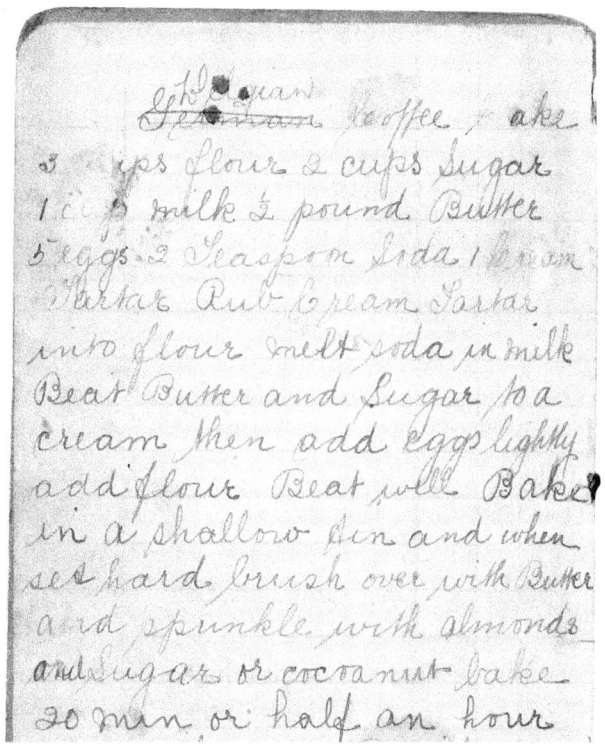

German Coffee Cake becomes Belgian Coffee Cake in Caroline Warner's handwritten recipe notebook 1912–1920.

The power of the radio

An appeal for early Anzac biscuit recipes was made on local 891 ABC Adelaide radio in April 2013. Listening in their Camden Park home were Judy and Bill Thomas, third generation custodians of a family recipe book. Judy was keen to reveal that 'her beloved Nan's handwritten cookbook dated back to 1909'. Judy's Nan, Isabel Elizabeth McAdam (1893–1980), lived in Penola in regional South Australia and started writing her recipe book at the age of 16. Handwritten on the inside cover was '1909' – the only date in the book. Therefore defining when, and over how long a period, the recipes were added has been challenging.

The book contained many country recipes, starting with Pickles – a first prize 'Adelaide Show Green Tomato Pickle', followed by 'Pickled Walnuts and Worcester Sauce' ('excellent' and 'very good' written alongside). Several pudding recipes followed, including the family plum pudding and Christmas pudding, recipes still made today. Biscuit recipes came much later in this book.

The first 146 recipes were numbered and this was helpful in ascertaining some possible dates of entries. Over 30 unnumbered recipes followed, some in a different hand but with comments written by Isabel. Some were local radio recipes (5DN and 5CL) and, typical of its time, the book included a miscellaneous section where hints about tanning leather, treating mange in dogs and how to plait a hide for a whip could be found.

A recipe that would help us date the entries came at 140 – 'Orange Sago', copied from the *Australian Woman's Mirror*, a weekly periodical published by the *Bulletin Newspaper* (Sydney) from 1924.

The Family Handwritten Recipe Book

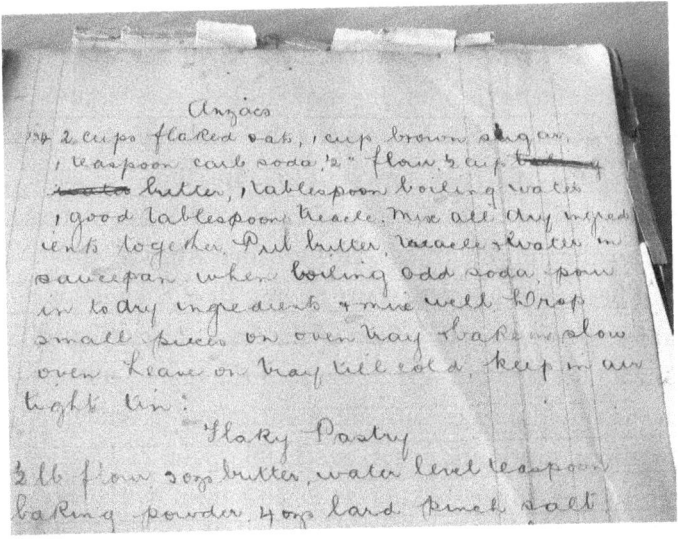

Munchies and Red Cross biscuits and Anzacs from Isabel Elizabeth McAdam's handwritten recipe book, 1909 to the mid-1920s.

Other *Mirror* recipes were added: 'Ginger Apples' at 145, 'Fig Conserve' at 146. Among the unnumbered recipes that followed, the first date recorded was for 'Aboriginal Gingerbread Prize Recipe' (*Mirror*, 12 May 1925). Although not accurate dating, it does give us a time period.

Later there is a recipe for 'Quince Jam Aunt Susan Cookbook'. This recipe came from *Aunt Susan's recipes: a collection of tried and palatable dishes – simple and economical* published in Adelaide by Vardon & Sons Ltd in 1920.

From this information we can surmise that the three consecutive biscuit recipes (132 to 134) found in the middle of this book were added prior to 1924/1925.

Munchies, Red Cross Biscuits and Anzacs

The first of these biscuits, 'Munchies', have similar ingredients to Anzacs as we know them, with only a slight variation in measurements and no coconut. The second, 'Red Cross Biscuits', are not unlike Anzacs, but are missing the vital ingredient of treacle or golden syrup. Here, brown sugar is specified and 'good dripping' is used instead of butter, and to finish they are topped with half an almond. The third recipe is called 'Anzacs'. This is important because it is the first use among all of the research material for the shortened version of the Anzac biscuit name. These Anzacs use brown sugar, the rest of the ingredients are the same as the Munchies with slight variations in amounts, and most importantly include a 'good tablespoon of treacle'. All three recipes advise baking in a 'slow oven' with extra instructions included in the recipe for Anzacs: 'leave on tray till cold and keep in an airtight tin'. This is good advice as this type of biscuit firms up when it is left to cool on a hot baking tray, and they store well and stay crisper if stored in an airtight tin. All three recipes included bicarbonate of soda dissolved in boiling water and were made the same way using the melting method. Noticeably, none of the recipes included coconut. Today, coconut is a significant ingredient and most Australians would not have tasted an Anzac without it. Family recipe books support the evidence that coconut was available; for example Caroline Warner's pre-1920 notebook included a recipe for 'Cocoanut Ice' and Isabel McAdam included 'Cocoanut Pudding'. However it was not an original ingredient in the earliest Anzac recipes.

Every crumb counts

The print media in South Australia, and elsewhere, promoted my public appeal for early Anzac biscuit recipes.

The prominent article headed *Battle of the Biscuit, every crumb counts in bid to solve Anzac mystery* on page 3 of the Adelaide *Advertiser* (20 April 2013) caught the attention of Heather Say's husband Stephen, from Mount Gambier. Knowing of Heather's family involvement in show cooking he 'kept prodding her' until she got in touch.

For many years, Heather's mother, Mavis Jean Wright (1925–2001), and grandmother, Esther May Jones (1895–1975), were show cooking judges in Mount Gambier and surrounding district shows. Esther's handwritten recipe book included a recipe for 'Red Cross Biscuits'. The recipe, like Isabel's, was without treacle or golden syrup. However, with the family being dairy farmers it was not surprising to see that Esther's recipe used butter instead of dripping and her recipe did not finish with the addition of half an almond.

Apart from family recipe books, it has been hard to find a Red

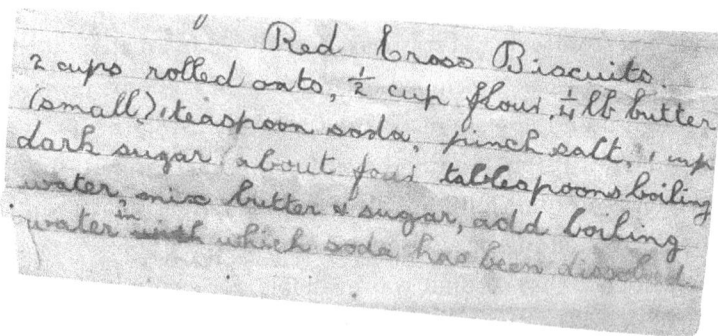

Pre-1915 recipe for Red Cross Biscuits from Esther May Jones (1895–1975), Heather Say's grandmother.

RED CROSS BISCUITS

One cup flour, 2 cups rolled oats, ½ lb. brown sugar, ¼ lb. clarified dripping, 1 teaspoon baking soda dissolved in 2 tablespoons boiling water. Mix dry ingredients, add melted dripping and soda, and stand to cool. Roll into small balls, put half an almond on each and bake in a slow oven.

'Red Cross Biscuits' in the *Goulburn Evening Penny Post* (NSW), 3 March 1930.

Cross biscuit recipe in a published cookery book. Most of the published recipes have been found in newspaper recipe columns. Were they just seen as wartime biscuits? Perhaps they were seen as too similar to the soldiers' biscuit? Undoubtedly, recipes for both were popular in newspapers during the Second World War.

Newspaper recipes top the Red Cross biscuit with half an almond, as Isabel McAdam did. The almond is not included on the soldiers' biscuit. Munchies and soldiers' biscuits have similarities with minor variations. However, soldiers' biscuits do have more similarities to Anzac biscuits than the Red Cross

Soldiers' Biscuits.—Cup plain flour, ½ cup sugar, large tablespoon treacle, heaped teaspoon carb. of soda, 2 cups John Bulls oats, cup butter, tablespoon boiling water. Put butter, treacle and water in large saucepan and bring them to the boil, then add soda and stir. Pour while still frothing into dry ingredients. Put out in teaspoon on greased tray, and make in a moderate oven. Leave on oven shelf until cold.

"HELEN."
ANZAC, OR SOLDIERS' BISCUITS.
2 cups flaked oats, 1 cup brown sugar (or white), 1 teaspoon soda, 1 cup plain flour, ½ cup butter, 1 or 2 tablespoons boiling water, 1 big tablespoon treacle or golden syrup. Mix all dry ingredients together, put butter, treacle, and water into a four-sized saucepan. When boiling add soda. Pour this mixture on the dry ingredients and mix well. Drop small pieces on greased tray and bake in a slow oven for about 15 to 20 minutes. Let them become cold before removing from tray.
E. LAWRENCE,
Suttontown.
Mrs. E. Penson uses 1 cup coconut and ½ cup flour, and only 1 cup oats.

Left: Soldiers' biscuit recipe from *Albury Banner and Wodonga Express*, NSW, 1930.
Right: Soldiers' biscuit recipe from a 1933 recipe book: *'From the south east of South Australia which is famous for everything including cookery'*, Back to Suttontown Recipe Book: five hundred selected recipes, Mt Gambier, South Australia.

biscuit. They both use brown sugar, but only the soldiers' biscuit adds treacle (unlike the golden syrup that is so distinctive in the Anzac). Good dripping or butter is used in both recipes and neither includes coconut.

Finding a recipe for soldiers' biscuits in a family recipe book has eluded me. However, there have been recipes published in cookery books and in newspaper recipe columns as the images above confirm.

Not only recipes are found in family recipe books

Remedies for health problems were also to be found in family recipe books, such as 'Onion Syrup for Colds' found in Caroline Warner's notebook. We have already mentioned some of the household hints written into Isabel's ledger book. These reveal the resourcefulness needed and the 'making do' experienced at times of war and austerity by this generation. However, I wasn't expecting to find a poem. At the very back of Isabel's ledger book, in the neatest handwriting, was a very long sad poem

> To My Sister (A. L. Gordon, 4 August 1853)
> Across the trackless seas I go,
> No matter when or where.
> And few my future lot will know,
> And fewer still will care.
> My hopes are gone, my time is spent,
> I little heed their loss,
> And if I cannot feel content,
> I cannot feel remorse.
>
> 2 My parents bid me cross the flood,
> My kindred frowned at me,
> They say I have belied my blood,
> And stained my pedigree.
> But I must turn from those who chide,
> And laugh at those who frown.
> I cannot quench my stubborn pride
> Nor keep my spirits down.
>
> 3 I once had talents, fit to win
> Success in life's career,
> And if I choose a part of sin,
> My choice has cost me dear.
> But those who brand me with disgrace,
> Will scarcely dare to say
> They spoke the taunt before my face,
> And went unscathed away.
>
> 4 My friends will miss a comrade's face,
> And pledge me on the seas,
> Who loved the wine cup or the chase,
> Or follies worse than these.

First four of 13 verses of a sad poem, 'To My sister (A.L. Gordon, 4 August 1853)' discovered at the back of Isabel McAdam's (ledger) handwritten recipe book, 1909.

(covering several ledger pages). The poem was entitled 'To My sister (A.L. Gordon 4 August 1853) going overseas and leaving home'. It was a heart-wrenching message to a sibling seeking a new life on the other side of the world. This handwritten poem is a wonderful example of a 'family keepsake' within another treasure – the family heirloom recipe book.

Chapter 7
Who Put the Coconut in the Anzac Biscuit?

Growing up in the northern hemisphere during the 1950s, I saw desiccated coconut as an exotic food that originated in tropical countries. It was a special ingredient used mainly in baking and confectionery. It was not until I was at catering college in the late 1960s that one of my flatmates introduced me to real 'English' curry, with all the accompaniments including coconut.

I moved to Darwin, Australia, in 1991. As a cook I was keen to bake Anzac biscuits for my first Anzac Day but had trouble finding a recipe (there was no Google in those days!). I asked the other mums at my son's primary school and a handwritten recipe was given to me on pretty Australian notepaper; it proudly remains in my personal baking file. In this recipe the biscuits are topped with an almond. Ironically, after purchasing the ingredients I found the recipe on the back of the golden syrup tin.

Nowadays around Anzac Day, many popular food magazines include articles on Anzac biscuits. They often offer something new or different. There are suggested variations that add other Australian ingredients, such as wattle seeds or macadamia nuts. One thing is certain, coconut is an embedded ingredient. But this hasn't always been the case.

Anzac Biscuits

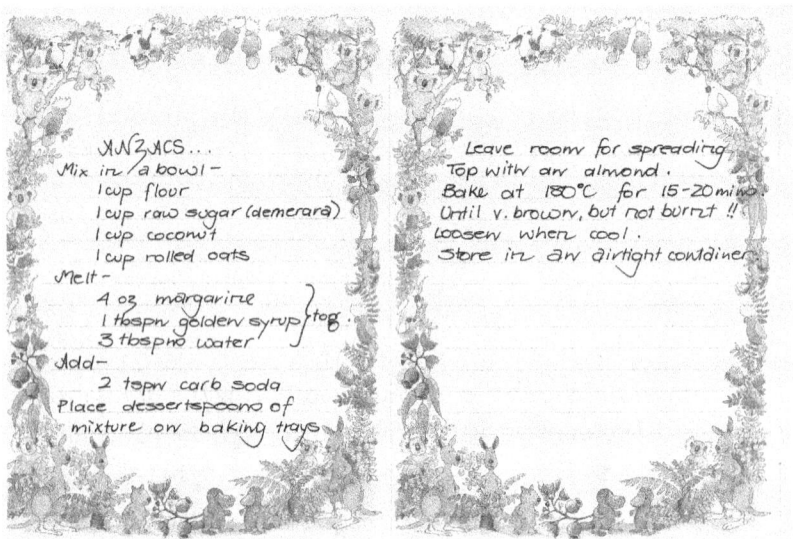

An Anzac Biscuit recipe from Bronnie Carson in Darwin.

'I have only ever known the Anzac biscuit with coconut,' insists my neighbour, Yvonne Baulderstone. As a South Australian farmer's wife, Yvonne regularly baked cakes and biscuits for morning and afternoon teas and her Anzacs are still family favourites. Naturally, I turn to Yvonne when I need to test Anzac biscuit recipes. Beth Farlam, a cookery book researcher and avid maker of Anzac biscuits agrees with Yvonne; Beth says, 'An Anzac's not an Anzac without the coconut.'

Most people are unaware that this defining ingredient was a late addition to the Anzac biscuit recipe. After researching published and handwritten family recipes we have discovered that Anzac biscuit recipes with and without coconut coexisted in the late 1920s and into the 1930s. By the Second World War – not long before Yvonne and Beth were introduced to their first

Anzac biscuits – coconut was a firmly established ingredient.

To date we haven't found a recipe that includes coconut in the ingredients before 1925. This is intriguing considering it is almost a decade after the Gallipoli landing. There is a general assumption that the First World War rationing had a lot to do with the absence of coconut, but many coconut recipes were found in pre-1920 Australian handwritten family recipe books, newspapers and published cookery books.

On the other hand, coconut was not used in the precursors to the Anzac biscuit, such as rolled oat biscuits, nutties, brownies, soldiers' biscuits, Red Cross biscuits and surprise biscuits, to name a few. Most importantly, the earliest published and handwritten recipes where the word 'Anzac' first appeared did not include coconut either.

Coconut facts

1. Barbara Santich writes in *Bold Palates, Australia's Gastronomic Heritage* that by the 1840s coconuts were on sale in Sydney. Desiccated coconut originated in Sri Lanka (then Ceylon) in 1880. It was imported into Australia in 28-pound tins from Ceylon and Fiji from 1885.

2. Stephanie Alexander in *The Cook's Companion* tells us that the coconut palm *Cocos nucifera* is native to Malaya but grows widely throughout the tropics. Her book tells us how to prepare a coconut and how to make coconut milk; she includes several curry recipes using coconut milk and a recipe for coconut ice using Copha (made from coconut oil). Surprisingly, there is no Anzac biscuit recipe in this book.

The 'Craze for Coconut'

In 2014, Australian gastronomy author Michael Symons writing for the *Australian Geographic* looked at 'what Australian cuisine means and how it's changed over the years'. Symons identified that Australian cookery books had lengthy sections on baking and he describes the popularity for coconut:

> An early craze for desiccated coconut showed up in Lamingtons and other innovations around the year 1900. Other Antipodean classics, such as Anzac biscuits, pumpkin scones, and Pavlova, came from this golden age of baking.

In her book *Bold Palates* Barbara Santich also writes about the 'Craze for Coconut': 'South Australia alone imported 100,000 pounds in 1909'. Much of that coconut would have been used for home baking and we find evidence of its popularity in early South Australian cookery books. South Australia was living up to its reputation as the 'Land of Cakes'. This endearing title was given to the State a decade earlier by the then governor's wife, Lady Victoria Buxton.

Evidence of the popularity of coconut recipes before 1920 can be found in the extensive baking sections of early Australian cookery books. For example, there are 14 in *The Kookaburra Cookery Book of Culinary and Household Recipes and Hints* (1911), 12 in *The Australian Household Guide* edited by Lady Hackett (1916) and 14 in *The Barossa Cookery Book* (1917). More coconut recipes appear in *The P.W.M.U. Cookery Book of Victoria* (1916), *The Cookery Book of Good and Tried Receipts* compiled for the Women's Missionary Association of the Presbyterian Church of New South Wales (14th edition, 1915) and *The Schauer Cookery Book* by Misses A. & M. Schauer, teachers of cookery and domestic arts, Brisbane Technical College (1909). Most of the coconut recipes use either the terms grated or desiccated cocoanut and occasionally cocoanut chips.

This is by no means a comprehensive list of all the cookery books of the time, but from these and other publications it is established that coconut was readily available and a popular ingredient during and after the First World War. Further proof of early coconut recipes can, of course, also be found in handwritten family recipe books prior to 1920.

> ### The Kookaburra Cookery Book cover changes
>
> The first edition of *The Kookaburra Cookery Book of Culinary and Household Recipes and Hints* was printed at Freason's printing house in 1911. The cover shows an Edwardian maid with a mob cap and a kookaburra behind her on a stand. The second edition was published by E.W. Cole in Melbourne in 1912. On the cover the maid no longer wears a mop cap and the kookaburra has moved to the chair. This edition contains a preface to the second edition and all additional recipes are added at the back.
>
> The third edition was printed in Melbourne by W.A. Comeadow Printer Pty Ltd in 1929. Reprints remained the same on the inside but confusingly the third cover change came much later, around the early 1940s, and depicts a young mother and child standing in front of a window from that time; on this cover the kookaburra has moved to the floor. Interestingly, the quality of the paper is poor compared to much earlier editions, telling us it was probably produced during the Second World War, or at least before 1946.

Lady Victoria Buxton and *The Kookaburra Cookery Book* connection

Lady Victoria Buxton (SA governor's wife, 1895–1898) was most impressed by the baking skills of the young ladies of South Australia. Her favourable comments were recorded in her biography Lady *Victoria Buxton: A Memoir with Some Account of her Husband* by the Right Hon. George W.E. Russell:

> This should be called 'Land of Cakes' by the way; the young ladies are remarkably good cake-and-scone makers and take much part in household work. There are cake stalls at all the numerous sales and strawberry fetes.

Due to Lady Buxton's delicate health her husband, Sir Thomas Fowell-Buxton, and their family returned to England before his five-year tenure expired. However, throughout their three years in Adelaide, Lady Buxton used her considerable vice-regal influence with the leading women of this society, 'wives of men bold', to establish The Lady Victoria Buxton Girls' Club in 1898. This club 'kept the girls off the streets' and was later able to move to premises offering much-needed accommodation for girls from the country seeking factory work in the city. A decade later, in order to purchase the neighbouring property and to boost its finances, the committee organised a fundraising cookery book. Ladies of the Adelaide Establishment and regional areas of South Australia were invited to submit recipes. This popular cookery book would be in continuous print from 1911 to 1929 and sent all over Australia. First published in Adelaide and later in Melbourne, the later editions included new recipes at the back of the book. Only the advertisements varied. The cover design changed three times (although the colour changed more often). These cover illustrations and the recipes within convey the considerable changes that took place in homes during these turbulent years.

Who Put the Coconut in the Anzac Biscuit?

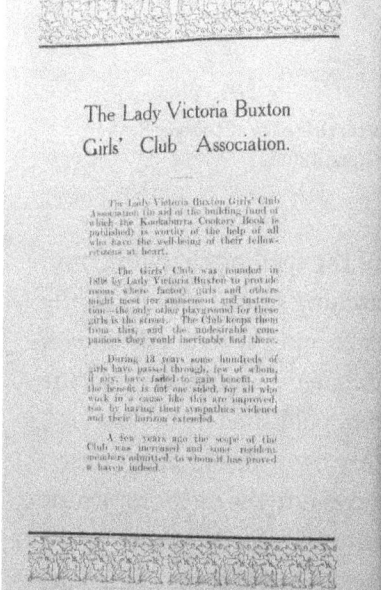 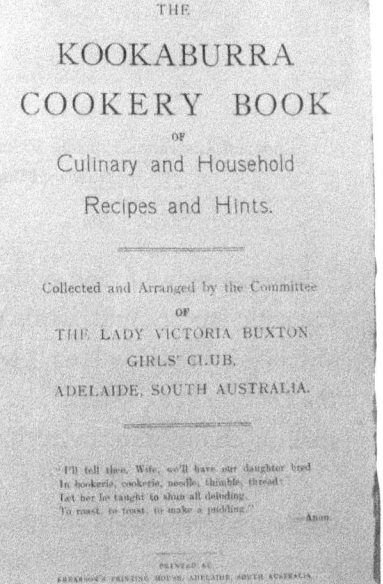

Cover and the title page (with reference to Lady Victoria Buxton's Girls Club) of *The Kookaburra Cookery Book of Culinary and Household Recipes and Hints* … including first edition 1911, and covers of 1912 and early 1940s editions.

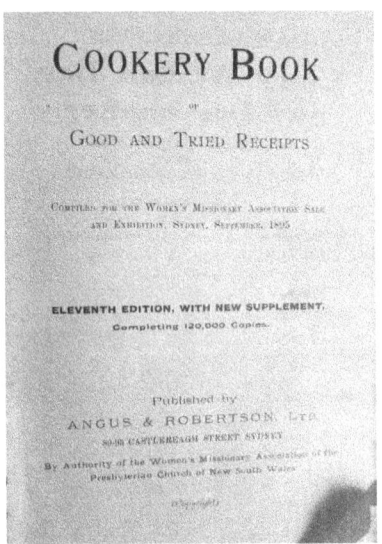

Cover of *Australian Household Guide*, 1916; title page of *Cookery Book of Good and Tried Receipts*, 1909.

Interestingly, I found evidence of the spelling changing from 'cocoanut' to 'coconut' while researching Anzac biscuits in the Mitchell Library, Sydney. I was examining several editions of *The Cookery Book of Good and Tried Receipts* and found that the spelling changed in the 19th edition, published in 1927.

Another South Australian cookery book, *Anchor Ann's Recipe Book*, was responsible for adding coconut to the recipe for Anzac biscuits a few years before the spelling changed. 'Anchor' was a trademark used by G. Wood & Co., wholesale grocers, merchants and manufacturers established in Adelaide (1854) and later in Port Adelaide, Fremantle, Broken Hill and London.

'Anchor Ann' was a pseudonym used by the company for the author of some of its cookery books and for demonstrations. A

Who Put the Coconut in the Anzac Biscuit?

Cover and recipe from
Anchor Ann's Recipe Book,
Adelaide, 1924/1925.

copy of *Anchor Ann's Recipe Book* that pre-dates the 1925 All–Australian Exhibition Special Issue includes an Anzac biscuit recipe with 'cocoanut'; unfortunately the date of publication is not confirmed. Cocoanut is still the preferred spelling for the coconut recipes found in *Anchor Ann's Recipe Book* 1934 edition, but surprisingly the Anzac biscuit recipe is no longer included.

The question is why was coconut not included in the early Anzac biscuit recipes? An important factor may have been that adding coconut might affect the keeping qualities of biscuits sent overseas. On the other hand, we could say, why was coconut added to the recipe years later?

Did grocers add coconut to the recipe in order to sell a fashionable ingredient from the grocery line? Or perhaps they just wanted to make the biscuit seem more antipodean. After all, since the turn of the century coconut had been a well-known ingredient in the Lamington Cake (as it was called in the first published recipe found in the *Queenslander* newspaper in 1902). Just as Anzac biscuits have today been shortened to 'Anzacs' the change to 'lamingtons' came later. But that's another intriguing Australian culinary story!

Chapter 8
Crispy versus Chewy
The eternal question

Does it matter?

Should Anzac biscuits be crispy or chewy? I am constantly asked this question whether I am giving an Anzac biscuit presentation to a local community group or undertaking one of the many radio interviews I give around Anzac Day.

In my opinion, much depends on early childhood experiences. If you have grown up eating homemade chewy Anzac biscuits then chewy Anzacs will be the ones you hanker after. On the other hand, supposing your grandmother or mother was a show cook? The chances are their Anzac biscuits would have been crisper, containing the essential snap that show judges look for, so a crunchy biscuit would probably be your preference. If some are destined for the biscuit tin then a crunchy style would also have better keeping qualities. Similarly, for the commercial market where a good shelf life is vital, crisper biscuits will stay firmer and fresher longer in the packet.

However, there's no doubt that homemade Anzac biscuits eaten straight from the cooling rack take some beating, while they still have a modicum of warmth and that divine sweet baking smell permeates the kitchen. Eaten soon after baking, they can be both crispy and crunchy on the outside and soft and chewy on the inside. (If reading this makes you want to bake a batch, go straight to pages 96 and 97 for the recipes.)

Cookery columns are popular in national and local newspapers. All sorts of recipes are requested by readers and the Anzac biscuit is often among them. I found evidence of an Anzac biscuit recipe request in a newspaper as early as 1916.

Recipes wanted

In the Kitchen and Pantry column of the Melbourne *Argus* (22 November 1916), reader 'O.N.' (Mornington) requests a recipe for 'quickly made biscuits'. Unlike Anzac biscuits, the recipe supplied includes an egg, but there are similarities in the making, the finishing technique and the baking. Like Anzacs, the melting method is used to combine the ingredients and the instructions say: 'Drop these biscuits in rough teaspoonfuls on a cool oven shelf, and bake in a moderate oven until evenly browned.'

The article then continues with this request: 'I should be glad if any of my readers could supply recipes for similar biscuits made with oatmeal and golden syrup . . .' That sounds more like an early Anzac biscuit recipe to me. Unfortunately, I was unable to find evidence that this recipe request was followed up.

A few years later (15 September 1920), a recipe for Anzac biscuits or crispies was sent in from 'Josephine' (E. Brunswick) and printed in the same Kitchen and Pantry column. Here John Bull oats were specified as an ingredient.

Within nine months (22 June 1921), the *Argus* published another Anzac biscuit recipe request. The column was headed Recipes Wanted and, squeezed between recipe requests for French toast, Coffee Scrolls and Steamed Cocoanut Pudding was the following: 'Jeanette' (Yarrawonga). John Bull or Anzac biscuits, made with John Bull oats, and including treacle; also Princess Pudding with apricot jam.'

RECIPES WANTED.

"Grateful" (Benalla).—French toast.
"Novice" (Bendigo).—Coffee scrolls made of cake and puff pastry mixture, and iced on top.
"Jeanette" (Yarrawonga).—John Bull or Anzac biscuits, made with John Bull oats, and including treacle; also princess pudding, with apricot jam.
"Housekeeper" (Melbourne).—Steamed cocoanut pudding.

'Jeanette' (Yarrawonga) under Recipes Wanted in the Melbourne *Argus*, 22 June 1921.

Two weeks later the requested recipe was printed (6 July 1921) in the Kitchen and Pantry column, this time under the heading Biscuits and Puddings: 'Caulfield' submitted two recipes including one for Anzac biscuits specifying John Bull oats.

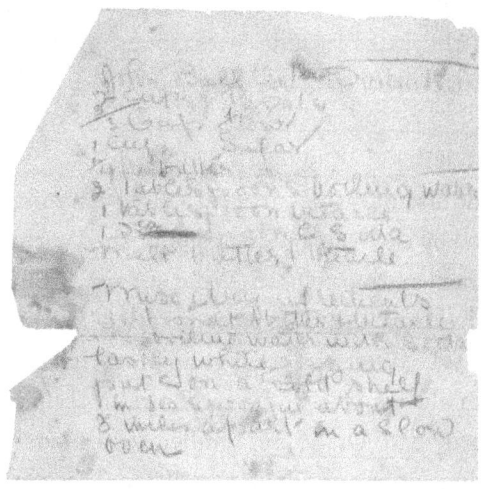

A recipe for John Bull Oat Biscuits (circa 1919) written in green crayon found in the family recipe book belonging to Annie Monfries (born 1889), grandmother of Jenny Fox.

A John Bull Oat Biscuits recipe was hastily written down using green crayon inside a family recipe book compiled by Annie Monfries of Wentworth in NSW circa 1919. Annie had passed the recipe on to her daughter Peggy Walton of the Adelaide Hills. Peggy was renowned among her friends as a good cook. These days Annie's granddaughter Jenny Fox is proud to have her grandmothers' handwritten recipe in the family archives.

A recipe for rolled oat biscuits using two 'breakfast' cupfuls of John Bull oats has been acknowledged to be a pre-cursor to the Anzac biscuit. A reader called Martin had been inspired by the article 'Australia strikes a blow in the battle for the Anzac biscuit' in the *Sydney Morning Herald* (January 2014), and used Trove to hunt for the recipe, which was then passed to the editor of the *Age*. This recipe had been found in the Queensland paper, *Warwick Examiner and Times*, dated 9 March 1912. The ingredients, method of making, and the baking are similar to Anzacs but they also include ½ teaspoon ginger – a popular additional ingredient in those days.

Nothing changes!

Today, Anzac biscuit recipes are still sought after in newspapers, as illustrated by the recipe requests published within six weeks of each other in the column What's Your Problem? in the Adelaide *Advertiser*. The first request is from 'P.L.' of Semaphore on 1 July 2014: 'What is a good recipe for Anzac biscuits? The ones I make always tend to be too hard.' A recipe from taste.com.au is provided. On 11 September 2014 reader 'J.M.' from Novar Gardens enquires about a traditional recipe, but also an 'Anzac biscuit recipe with orange as an ingredient', and other variations as well.

For the traditional recipe the newspaper column refers the reader to a recipe listed on the Australian War Memorial website as a popular version. It is from an original recipe provided by Mr Lawson, an Anzac soldier present at the Gallipoli landing. Efforts to find out more about Bob Lawson and his original recipe were unsuccessful.

The newspaper article also lists a number of variations and substitutions for creating flavour and texture, such as using wholemeal flour, brown sugar (very popular), chopped almonds, vanilla, orange juice or lemon juice.

Why do we feel the need to change or add things to the original recipe? Is it necessary? If we must, then why not give the alternative or adapted biscuit recipe a different name. By all means add other ingredients – just don't call them Anzac biscuits. The Anzac biscuit is special and the recipe deserves to be respected.

Changing the recipe

You have probably gathered by now that I am not in favour of changing classic or iconic recipes. As a professional cook, a cookery teacher for many years, and as a culinary historian I am a firm believer in keeping the integrity of the original recipe or dish where possible. I know a wartime economy recipe may be improved with extra butter, eggs or even sugar and that is fine when it is at least acknowledged. But where do we draw the line when it comes to the Anzac biscuit? What about the coconut? If I was being pedantic, I would say that coconut was not in the original recipe. As I wrote in an earlier chapter, coconut was first added a decade after Gallipoli, around 1925.

Crispy and Chewy Anzac Biscuits

Some like Anzacs crispy while others like Anzacs chewy. Now you can please everyone. It seems we had a sweeter tooth in days gone by! It is possible to reduce the sugar by up to ½ cup without it affecting either recipe too much.
Pre heat oven to 170°C/325°F/150°C fan-forced/Gas 3
Line two baking trays with baking parchment or lightly oil.

Crispy Anzac Biscuits

1 level cup/145 g/4½ oz plain flour
1 cup/90 g/3 oz rolled oats (not instant)
1 cup/70 g/2½ oz desiccated coconut
1 cup/200 g/7 oz sugar (granulated sugar is good for crispy)
125 g/4½ oz butter
2 x 20 mL tablespoons golden syrup (open lid and stand the tin in bowl of hot water to soften the syrup before measuring)
1 teaspoon bicarbonate of soda (bicarb)
2 tablespoons boiling water (water must be boiling when you use it)

- Mix flour, oats, desiccated coconut and sugar in a large bowl. Melt butter in a large pan over moderate heat, add golden syrup (dip tablespoon in hot water before measuring), stir till dissolved, bring gently to boiling point then remove pan from heat.
- Mix boiling water and bicarb and stir till dissolved. Add this to the hot melted mixture and stir till it froths up the pan.
- Carefully add the frothy mixture to the dry ingredients and mix well. If a little dry, add ½ tablespoon of extra water to help bind it together.
- Take a rounded dessertspoon of the mixture and roll into a ball. Place on baking trays 5 cm apart, the biscuits will spread.
- Press biscuits down using a fork, the back of spoon, or the bottom of a cup measure. Put trays in the oven.
- After 15 minutes take trays (1 tray at a time) out of the oven and press biscuits flat again.
- Return trays to the oven and continue baking for a further 3 to 4 minutes or until golden (they will still be soft).
- Leave the biscuits on the trays to firm up until completely cool, about 10 minutes.

This recipe makes 25-28 biscuits.

Chewy Anzac Biscuits

½ level cup/75 g/2½ oz plain flour
½ level cup/75 g/2½ oz self-raising flour
1 cup/90 g/3 oz rolled oats (not instant)
1 cup/70 g/2½ oz desiccated coconut
1 cup/200 g/7 oz sugar (try half caster and half soft brown sugar)
125 g/4½ oz butter
1 x 20 mL tablespoon of golden syrup. (Open lid and stand the tin in bowl of hot water to soften before measuring.)
1 teaspoon bicarbonate of soda (bicarb)
1 tablespoon boiling water. (You may need to add a little extra water when you bind the ingredients together so that you can form a ball in your hand.)

- Mix flours, oats, desiccated coconut and sugar in a large bowl. Melt the butter in a large pan over medium heat, add golden syrup (dip tablespoon in hot water before measuring), stir till dissolved, bring gently to boiling point then remove pan from heat.
- Mix boiling water and bicarb and stir till dissolved. Add this to the hot melted mixture and stir till it froths up the pan.
- Carefully add the frothy mixture to the dry ingredients and mix well. If a little dry add ½ tablespoon of extra water to help bind it together.
- Take a rounded dessertspoon of mixture, roll into a ball. Place balls on baking trays 5 cm apart, the biscuits will spread.
- Press biscuits down using a fork, the back of spoon, or the bottom of a cup measure. Place trays in oven.
- After 15 minutes take trays (1 tray at a time) out of the oven and press biscuits flat again.
- Return trays to oven and continue baking for a further 3 to 4 minutes or until golden brown (they will be soft).
- Leave the biscuits on the trays for barely a minute – just enough time for the biscuits to firm up slightly before transferring them to a wire rack to finish cooling.

This recipe makes 26-30 biscuits.

Once cooled, store these delicious biscuits, crispy or chewy, in an airtight tin.

Recipes came from far and wide

When friends knew I was writing about the Anzac biscuit there was no stopping the recipes from trickling in. Many of my Australian baking friends swear by the *Australian Women's Weekly* recipe, others always use the *Woman's Day* recipe. Then again, there are some who prefer Margaret Fulton's version. I even found an Anzac biscuit recipe on a tea towel in my local post office at Crafers in the Adelaide Hills.

Friends Gilly and Julia passed on Anzac biscuit recipes from their more recent editions of New Zealand's longest running cookery book the *Edmonds Sure to Rise Cookery Book* (first published in 1907 by the Edmonds Baking Powder Company). Ann-Marie Kennedy (Auckland University of Technology) in *Marketing's influence on the food culture of a nation: As told through the Edmonds' Cookery Book* wrote: 'Curiously, another of New Zealand's iconic foods, the Anzac biscuit, is not featured in the cookbook (5th edition, 1922).' Kennedy went on to state that recipes for the Anzac biscuit and that other iconic national food – the pavlova – were finally added to the 6th edition Edmonds cookbook in 1945.

'A few chopped walnuts are an improvement to classic Anzac ingredients' says New Zealand writer and curator Alexa Johnston in a more recent baking publication, *Ladies, a Plate: Traditional Home Baking* (2008). Johnston gives two Anzac biscuit recipes – a classic recipe for today and a 1933 recipe that includes walnuts, but no rolled oats. I came across this gem of a New Zealand baking book (which has a good section on recipe history) while browsing in the Dunedin University Bookshop.

Nuts were a popular addition to Anzac biscuit recipes by Australian home cooks too. One such recipe was found in

Crispy versus Chewy

Sallie Heysen's (1879–1962) Anzac biscuit recipe, with almonds.

Sallie Heysen's collection; Sallie was the wife of landscape painter Hans Heysen and was renowned for her hospitality and baking skills. She probably included these biscuits along with her famous honey biscuits when sending care packages to her daughter Nora (the first Australian woman to serve as a war artist in WWII) and to Nora's two younger brothers who were serving in the RAAF at the time.

Eilleen from Queensland drew my attention to the Anzac biscuit recipe in *Classic Country Cooking: Traditional Australian Fare*. The author, Lady Flo Bjelke-Petersen, a senator in the 1980s and wife of the Queensland premier, was famous in national folklore for her pumpkin scones. Writing about Anzac biscuits she says: 'Lovely biscuits made all the better by the addition of Kingaroy peanuts' – crediting an addition from her hometown.

Jenny from Darwin sent me a copy of her English mum's early 1970s *Biscuits Galore: W.I. Recipes* (Women's Institute UK). This too included a recipe for ANZACS (Australian Cookies), with the ingredients including chopped raisins.

Another recipe made its way to me on a postcard from New South Wales courtesy of Hawkesbury Cruises 'specialising in Seniors' Day trips'. I gather that Ben's Anzac biscuits are most welcome with a cuppa on the riverboat trip. Thanks Annette for passing it on.

UK expats Michael and Audrey Kent attended a talk I gave to the Historical Society of South Australia in 2014. As subscribers to the *Dalesman*, a monthly magazine from northern England, they soon shared with me the August edition which contained an Anzac biscuit recipe on Mrs Simkins' Country Kitchen page. With not a cup measure in sight, Mrs Simkins writes 'here is a version of those biscuits, prepared with slightly different proportions, giving more of a softer cookie consistency: they are ideal to carry with you for a tramp around the Dales'.

Libby Shore of Mount Barker made the Anzac biscuits for the Combined Hills History Groups' meeting in Stirling in April 2014, at which I was a guest speaker. I discovered later the delicious chewy treacly texture was due to brown sugar and extra golden syrup. Libby sent me her recipe on a gumleaf notelet – a lovely Aussie touch.

With the renewed interest in baking through reality TV shows there is no shortage of baking books full of traditional and modern baking recipes. However, expediency often means people turn to the internet to source a quick recipe reference. Be warned – you can have too much of a good thing. A quick search turned up more than I bargained for.

Crispy versus Chewy

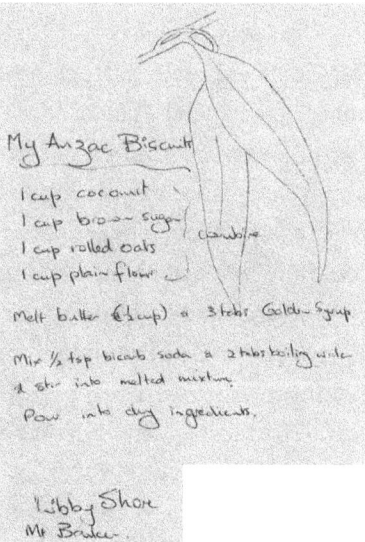

'My Anzac Biscuits' recipe on gumleaf paper from Libby Shore, member of Combined Hills History Group, Mt Barker, 2014.

Online videos – a touch of hit and miss

If you need advice on baking Anzac biscuits then YouTube will confuse you further, there are just too many to choose from. Here's a few to get you started!

Good Chef Bad Chef lost me the minute they called them Anzac cookies. Eventually the finished biscuits were sandwiched together with ice cream; I'm sure these 'cookies' made a nice dessert. *One Pot Chef's* mixture turned out very stiff, more water was needed. No wonder they referred to the spoonfuls as 'globs'. *Cooking with Karma* used brown sugar and pressed down the uncooked biscuits with a fork before baking them (no problem with that, it's good for the chewy variety, but for a flatter crisper biscuit I recommend a flat-based item such as a cup measure). *Keep Calm and Bake* added all the ingredients to the pan in one go including the bicarbonate of soda. Bicarbonate is normally dissolved in hot water before being added to the other ingredients.

However, one of the better instructional videos was given by chef Tobie Puttock. Puttock promotes Jamie Oliver's Anzac biscuit recipe, which has been adapted and includes orange juice and vanilla extract. Can we forgive a famous British chef for tweaking our Anzac biscuit recipe? Maybe this was the citrus recipe that J.M. from Novar Gardens was searching for.

To be fair, I have not baked and tested all these online recipes so I cannot say how well they turn out. But, I did note that among the five online examples I watched there were variations in cooking temperatures from 160°C–180°C and baking time from 10–20 minutes. Therefore it's a bit of a gamble choosing an online recipe to follow. For step-by-step video instructions try the giant chewy Anzac biscuits promoted by CSR (Colonial Sugar Refining Company) with or without the upsize and the added cinnamon. It appears that everyone including CSR wants to 'give a twist to this Aussie/Kiwi classic' for there are seven different Anzac biscuit recipes on the CSR website. Among them are recipes that use rice flour and olive oil spread. Another version uses low GI cane sugar, and for extra crunchy biscuits there's a recipe which uses plain white sugar, extra oats and walnuts.

In many of their recipes, CSR suggests mixing different sugars as well as generous amounts of golden syrup. Obviously, as an Australian company for over 160 years and producers of sugar and golden syrup they do have a vested interest. However, the mixing of the sugars is a nice idea; the castor provides the crunch, while the lovely toffee flavour, moisture and chewiness come from using brown sugar and golden syrup. These ingredients also give the baked biscuit an attractive golden colour.

CSR have also produced a recipe card showing Anzac biscuits sandwiched together with a decadent chocolate cream; they say the combination is 'a match made in flavour heaven'. The sugar used here is demerara, which would ensure extra crunch. CSR also recommend that you 'try an orange or lemon buttercream for a wonderful citrus balance to the sweet Anzac biscuit'.

Talking of sweetness and balance, it seems we don't have as sweet a tooth as we used to have. Australian food identity Maggie Beer likes her Anzacs thin and crisp and, yes, of course, she gives a little adaptation too. 'A little lemon rind to counter the sweetness' is the ingredient Maggie 'sneaks in' (Simon Wilkinson's words). In a full-page article 'Sweet Taste of Home' (*Advertiser* 22 April 2015) Simon stresses Maggie's understanding of the emotional connection to the creation of the Anzac biscuit. He quotes Maggie as saying 'it's a recipe born of love and necessity ... Those little luxuries from home would have meant so much'.

Well said, Maggie! They say necessity is the mother of invention and these days finding a gluten-free recipe is also a consideration for many. I doubt there would have been a call for gluten-free Anzac biscuits all those years ago.

No one need miss out

In 2017, gluten-free products are available on supermarket shelves all around Australia, at farmers' market stalls and specialist grocery providores. Gluten-free cakes and biscuits also adorn the glass display stands on café counters. More often than not, the homemade 'bring a plate' community gatherings and work morning teas will now have more than orange and almond cake for the allergy challenged. I came across a gluten-free Anzac biscuit recipe when I was a guest at an Anzac Centenary theatre production at Bridgewater Primary School in 2015. I had recently met the students and teachers baking Anzac biscuits together. On this occasion the parents and students provided the interval refreshments of tea and Anzac biscuits. Jane had brought along her home-baked gluten-free Anzac biscuits; the recipe devised so her family could enjoy Anzac biscuits. Luckily I managed to sample one before they were all snapped up.

Developing recipes

Early in my research into the Anzac biscuit story I tested more recipes for this iconic biscuit than I care to mention. A spreadsheet of the similarities, differences, variations and so much more was compiled from Australian magazines and popular cookbooks. These confirmed that the amount of butter was the only constant ingredient. There were variations in the dry ingredients (oats, flour, sugar and coconut) of half a cup to two cups, the bicarbonate of soda from a quarter to two teaspoons, and the water and the golden syrup from one to two tablespoons. The range in the cooking temperature and baking times were also considerable: 150°C–180°C for anywhere between 10 and 20 minutes.

The tried and tested recipes included on pages 96 and 97 evolved after much testing (thank you to Yvonne and Beth). It also provides the cooking tips that will give you a crispy or a chewy version.

Passing on the family recipe

If you want to win prizes for your Anzacs then you really can't go further than the advice of a show judge whose family recipe has been around for four generations. South Australian show judge Susan Rabbitt, who has been exhibiting in shows for over

Crispy versus Chewy

ANZAC BISCUITS

Slow oven. + Hot

1 cup Rolled Oats
1 " Flour
1 " Sugar
¾ cup Coconut
1 Tablespoon Golden Syrup
4 ozs Butter or Margarine
2 Tablespoons Boiling Water
1½ Teaspoons B.Carb of Soda

In a large bowl mix rolled oats, flour & sugar & coconut. Put golden syrup & butter or margarine into a saucepan & place over gentle heat until melted. Measure boiling water into a bowl, add bicarb of soda & then stir into melted ingredients. Add to the dry ingredients in bowl & stir until mixed. Brush trays with melted butter & spoon dessertspoonfuls of mixture on trays about 2" apart to allow for spreading. Bake in mod slow oven 20 minutes. Remove from oven leave a few seconds to set and lift off trays with spatula. Cool on a rack. Store in an air tight tin.

170°C m—y ST.
New trays - 15 min

Susan's 1930s Anzac Biscuit recipe in her mother's handwriting. Susan has added oven temperatures (in pencil) from different ovens she has used. The recipe is now used regularly by granddaughter Michailey.

30 years, knows what it's like to compete. She became involved in stewarding and judging eight years ago as a way of 'giving back to the show'. She spent the first two years as a shadow judge learning from the esteemed SA show-cooking judge Margaret Hurst. Susan stresses the importance of storing biscuits in airtight tins not plastic boxes, as it keeps the biscuits fresher and crisper.

Susan has always used her mother's 1930s Anzac biscuit recipe. Winifred Ivy Phillips (née Rice) was born on 6 July 1913, just before the First World War, and was married in 1941. It is likely that Winifred baked Anzac biscuits throughout the Second World War. In 1969 her handwritten recipe was given to her daughter Susan along with other family favourites as part of a wedding present. Recently, Susan passed the family recipe on to her daughter Michailey, who now bakes her grandmother's Anzac biscuit recipe with her own children. Apparently, the biscuits are both crispy and chewy. No wonder this recipe has stood the test of time.

Chapter 9

Show Cooking and the Anzac Biscuit

Who doesn't love a good show?

During my childhood in England, one of the highlights of summer was the annual Heytesbury Village Flower Show, an opportunity for my father (a market gardener) to demonstrate his horticultural skills. The whole family prepared for the show weeks beforehand. I wonder now how my mother managed to organise (and afford) for six children to enter so many different junior classes. There was always handwriting to practice and labour over; wildflowers to collect, press and display; a piece of craftwork or a drawing to finish; a matchbox collection to sort and mount; and, on the day of the show, the miniature garden on a tray to create. My favourite activity was baking for the cooking classes. We would all get up early on show day to put the final touches to our entries. Fortunately, most of my mother's entries were in the preserve classes so her individual raspberry, blackcurrant or strawberry jam had already been cleaned up and labelled ready to exhibit. On show day, my mother would supervise my attempts at scones and a handmade Victoria sandwich. All these baked goods required different oven temperatures – not easy to accomplish in our temperamental Rayburn wood-burning stove! All sorts of activities would be taking place at the show held in the grounds of Heytesbury

Anzac biscuit entries in a glass showcase with
Royal Adelaide Show (RAS) blue ribbons, 2012.

House. However, not even the swing boats (the only children's rides), or the annual gymkhana taking place in the adjoining field, could distract me from the show exhibitors' tent. Once the entries were in and judging was underway the excitement mounted. Regardless of the results, it was always an enjoyable and memorable day. I still love a good show, who doesn't? Whether in the UK or Australia, I still make a beeline for the cookery sections, and in no time those childhood memories come flooding back.

Show Cooking and the Anzac Biscuit

In Australian shows, the cookery classes maintain their traditional baking favourites: scones (including pumpkin scones), various sponges (like the blow-away and ginger fluff), and other cakes such as sultana, Genoa, and boiled and rich fruit cakes. These days, shows include items that reflect trends in baking such as the friand, macaron and the revived cupcake. In most shows biscuits have featured in the cookery sections as a separate class; some biscuits have disappeared only to be revived years later. To discover how the Anzac biscuit has been represented in show cookery I sent a survey to the eight State and Territory Royal shows.

There are simply hundreds of agricultural/horticultural shows throughout Australia, so for the purpose of this book I limited my enquiries to the State and Territory capital shows. In all the capital cities the Royal or statewide agricultural/horticultural societies manage large showgrounds and hold a show that lasts several days. As Royal shows are relatively new in Australia I felt that a brief description of the history of show societies in Australia might be useful.

Show history: the growth of towns and the establishment of shows

According to the survey 'Agricultural Shows in Australia', undertaken in 1999 by Kate Darian-Smith and Sara Wills, agricultural shows were established throughout the 1800s as townships grew around the country. They suggest that the goldrush in Victoria, population increase in New South Wales, and the optimism of Federation in 1901 all contributed to this development. In South Australia, by 1910, towns were growing as a result of village irrigation schemes, and, later, soldier settlements after WWI.

The survey also highlights problems, such as droughts, pests and rabbit plagues, which may have caused a decline in the establishment of shows during the 1890s. In the 1930s the number of shows fell dramatically due to the Depression. In addition, many existing agricultural shows did not operate during the First or Second World Wars. A surge in interest in shows caused an increase in the 1980s, but interestingly the number of shows decreased during the 1990s. More recently there has once again been a resurgence.

Respecting heritage and preserving tradition

Cookery sections came much later in the life of most capital shows; today, some include biscuit classes and some do not. Over the years the Anzac biscuit, or its precursors (with names such as nutties or rolled oat biscuits), may have made an appearance under 'assorted biscuits' or a 'mixed plate of biscuits'. Surprisingly, a specific Anzac biscuit class did not appear until the mid-1990s and then not in all the Royal shows. The cookery section committee at the Royal Darwin Show (RDS) decided to promote the Anzac biscuit for the 60th anniversary in 2011. The members considered it an important part of Australian culture and history and wanted to encourage future generations to continue to cook the biscuits. The Darwin Country Women's Association (CWA) supported this wholeheartedly and contributed extra prize money.

Many regional shows in cities, country towns and the bush do include the Anzac biscuit in their cookery classes, especially in the junior sections. Long may they continue to do so, the shows after all, among many other aims, are about respecting heritage and preserving tradition!

Special cookery for the Anzac Centenary

During 2015, three capital Royal shows – Canberra, Perth and Melbourne – paid tribute to the Anzac Centenary by including cookery classes with generous prizes. Naturally, they all included Anzac biscuits, as well as other iconic Australian fare such as lamingtons, damper and the boiled fruit cake.

Australian Capital Territory: The Royal Canberra Show (RCS) – 'Commemorating the Gallipoli Diggers'

The Royal Canberra Show takes place in February, close to Anzac Day, so I was not surprised to discover that this show, from Australia's national capital, had paid tribute to the 'Diggers of Gallipoli', holding their cooking class in the Harvest Hall. For this special class the 28 entrants baked six Anzac biscuits, six lamingtons and one plain damper.

The Royal Canberra Show: the schedule promoting the Anzac biscuit class.

Western Australia: ANZAC Remembrance for the Perth Royal Show (PRS)

For 2015 only, the organisers of the Perth Royal Show added an ANZAC Remembrance class in the cookery section, to include 'Anzac biscuits (6), Shortbread (6), 15 cm Boiled Fruit Cake, and an energy bar . . . The exhibitors are to provide a suitable box or tin to display entry'.

The Anzac biscuit is the food most often identified with Anzac commemorations. The addition of shortbread acknowledges Australia's Scottish baking heritage, the inclusion of the boiled fruit cake a nod to the popularity of this 1930s economical and speedily made Australian fruit cake. The energy bar would be seen as an on trend element, indicative of the rise in 'on the go' food today.

Victoria: 'The Great Anzac Biscuit Challenge' at the Royal Melbourne Show (RMS)

The Royal Melbourne Show's 2015 Anzac Biscuit Challenge sought to preserve the old and introduce the new. It promoted creativity and a modern twist on an Australian classic. Especially for the Anzac Centenary, the show included new classes in the Art, Craft and Cookery competition. In the open class there were two categories: the Contemporary Challenge Anzac Biscuit and the Commemorative Biscuit. For the contemporary challenge the design brief states:

> Using the traditional Anzac biscuit as a base, adapt the recipe to include different flavours and ingredients – for example, quinoa, chia seeds, macadamia nuts – to create a modern twist on the Australian classic. (Batch of four biscuits.)

For the commemorative biscuit:

> Produce an original biscuit that creatively represents the commemoration of the Anzac Centenary (Batch of four biscuits.) For example, biscuits could be poppy-shaped, iced in the shape of poppies, contain poppy seeds or other ways to represent the commemoration of the centenary.

Secondary school students (years 7–12) have their own class for the Anzac cooking challenges.

Commemorative biscuits entered in the Anzac Biscuit Challenge, Royal Melbourne Show, 2015.

Spare a thought for the cooking class judges as they snap the biscuits, taste test and then decide on the best in show.

Show judging – all a matter of following the show guidelines

Regardless of their individual preferences cooking-class judges are first and foremost guided by the show guidelines. The Royal Adelaide Show (RAS) gives strict guidelines. These state that Anzac biscuits must be an even, deep golden colour (no burnt bottoms!) and they must be even in size and shape and not oversize (there are normally five biscuits exhibited per plate). The biscuits must taste good; they should be evenly mixed with no evidence of undissolved soda and they must snap when broken. In order to snap, the biscuits need to be crispy and this can be a problem in some shows. Pam Hamill, chief steward of the Royal Darwin Show cookery section, stresses the difficulties facing the Territory competitors:

> The climate plays a large part in the success or failure of the biscuit. If the weather is unseasonably humid the biscuits will be soggy; if we are having the usual dry season weather of clear days and coldish nights the biscuits will be superb.

Does size matter?

The Royal Queensland Show (RQS) based in Brisbane specifies that Anzac biscuits 'must not be café sized', i.e. between six and eight centimetres. In Adelaide the guidelines say 'not over-sized', but like most shows, give no measurements. In recent years, extra-large Anzac biscuits have become popular following the fashion in coffee shops and cafés for serving larger portions. This trend is in keeping with the extra-large American chocolate-chip cookies and the Australian cornflake biscuits that dominate the glass jars on café counters.

To assist exhibitors some shows (such as the Royal Melbourne Show) give an Anzac biscuit recipe. Despite this, the biscuits exhibited can be quite diverse in shape, colour and taste. Country show judges like to encourage entries. Judges are not compelled to give a first or second place if the biscuits are not up to standard. It's a different matter with the Royal shows; 'Royal has to be best' stresses Royal Adelaide Show cooking judge Susan Rabbitt, 'near enough is not going to do it for you'. However, when Susan was invited to judge the Anzac biscuit classes at the July 2015 Royal Darwin Show she found the high humidity had played havoc with the Anzac biscuits and allowances were made for this unavoidable climatic disadvantage.

How these specific judging guidelines came about no one seems to know. We do know that the precursors to the Anzac biscuit needed to be crisp in order to travel well. Crisp biscuits stay fresh longer and would last the two-to-three-month sea voyage during the First World War.

The inclusion of the Anzac biscuit in shows acknowledges its significance in the history of Australia, helps keep the Anzac spirit alive, and provides us with a window into Australia's past and present culinary history.

I am indebted to the author Liz Harfull for this tale, included in her award-winning publication *The Blue Ribbon Cookbook*:

> The Penola Show (in the south-east of South Australia) ingeniously involved the local RSL branch and WWII diggers in choosing the best biscuits baked by school students, and, with a $50 winner's prize, there was no shortage of student entries. The diggers enjoyed the biscuits so much that in the process of judging they ate all the winner's biscuits. The steward returned to find only crumbs to put on show!

Chapter 10
Keeping the Anzac Spirit Alive

There are many ways in which the Anzac spirit of caring and looking out for each other continues. Food and in particular the Anzac biscuit is used to convey acts of kindness and caring, as demonstrated by Baked Relief; as a way of connecting with home for expats living abroad; and in the form of commemoration and remembering in the collectors' biscuit tins.

These are only three of many possible examples; three personal stories, which I feel demonstrate the ongoing importance of the spirit of the ANZACs.

Baked Relief – feeding hearts

Baked Relief is a simple and selfless idea to support those in need. It demonstrates that the Anzac biscuit is more than the baking, more than the community giving; it's about rallying together when others are in need. By doing this, the Anzac biscuit becomes a powerful symbol, a way of making a difference. Danielle Crismani's inspirational story shows us what one person can achieve. Donating home-baked food rather than filling sandbags was Danielle's answer to helping her local Brisbane SES (State Emergency Services) during the severe Queensland floods in 2011. This simple act of home baking had a profound impact on the emergency team.

Offers to help with the baking poured in after Danielle posted details on social media. The level of support that followed surprised even Danielle and encouraged her to instigate the direct giving network Baked Relief. Danielle says that she and others found it was a way of making a difference, of contributing to disaster relief through baking.

In 2014 Baked Relief members once again saw a need in the plight of the Queensland drought-stricken farmers and they responded in a similar way. The call to bake went out and 'Love to the West' was created.

Farmers are still battling for survival. By 2015, 90 per cent of Queensland was drought-declared and the members of Baked Relief decided it was once again time to show farmers the spirit of mateship. Homemade fruit cakes and Anzac biscuits were baked and wrapped, handwritten messages were attached, and these gifts of love were sent out west to the Queensland farming families just in time for Anzac Day 2015. This act of kindness was a positive way for city folk to show they cared, that they understood times were tough in the bush for farmers and their families.

Acknowledging the farmers' role in our nation's food security by sending them food is indeed powerful. The significance is amplified by the use of the Anzac biscuit. Just as the women on the home front baked and posted food to soldiers over a century ago, people today bake biscuits from store-cupboard ingredients. Whether the recipient is a soldier or a farmer's family, Anzac biscuits embody Australianness, conveying the Anzac spirit of courage, endurance, survival and mateship and, what's more, 'they taste bloody good too'.

Anzacs provided by Baked Relief in 2014 – with a poem.

The Australia and New Zealand Association

After six years as an expatriate living in Hong Kong, I can identify with the lengths that expats will go to when searching for a vital ingredient to bring about that taste of home. I came across this story of the search for golden syrup for Anzac biscuits from a member of the Australia and New Zealand Association (ANZA) living in Indonesia.

Partners of expatriate workers in Indonesia are not allowed to have paid employment. ANZA provides an organisation for Australian and New Zealand expatriate partners to meet socially and to raise funds for social welfare in Indonesia. Twice a year, in May and November, the Indonesian ANZA group hold The Bazaar, their major fundraiser, to support the many social welfare programs and projects undertaken by ANZA throughout the year. Jakarta ANZA member Gilly Weaver tells me that the bazaars are a huge drawcard, 'people rush in to buy the traditional things that they no longer make at home'. Anzacs,

Afghans, lamingtons and melting moments (all made by ANZA members) disappear from the cake stall in no time. As Gilly says 'people living overseas love a bit of home'.

The Australian and New Zealand Association (ANZA) biannual bazaar cake stall with banner, Jakarta, Indonesia, 2015.

Golden syrup is hard to find in Indonesia. Now and then, expensive small tins are available in Western supermarkets, but many members rely on their supplies being met from visiting friends and relatives who are asked to bring golden syrup. The call then goes out among the membership to see who has golden syrup for Anzacs. Home bakers who have tried substituting honey or extra sugar for the golden syrup know only too well that the secret to a good Anzac lies in the golden syrup.

It is not just the ingredients that contribute to a successful Anzac biscuit. Many home ovens in Indonesia have no convection and get intensely hot; consequently burnt batches of biscuits are common. ANZA members have taught a local Indonesian, Usni, to make Anzac biscuits in her café in ANZA House, the venue for committee meetings, activities and weekly gatherings since 1994. Usni knows how important it is to have freshly baked Anzac biscuits and hers are café-style – the large and chewy kind.

Usni with Anzac biscuits in the ANZA café, Jakarta, Indonesia, in 2015.

Taking the biscuit – Anzac biscuits and the collectors' tins

My addiction to collecting biscuit tins started in England in the late 1960s. The first, a tall, red McVitie's Digestive biscuit tin, was hotly followed by a slimmer blue McVitie's Rich Tea biscuit tin. I blame this infatuation on my college friend and flatmate Herbie, who encouraged me and our flatmates Sue and Meriel to devour these sweet, moreish biscuits on a regular basis. Since living in Australia, Arnott's biscuit tins have found their way into my collection and over the last few years I have added the Unibic commemorative Anzac biscuit tins.

In 2002, Unibic produced a limited edition biscuit tin to coincide with Anzac Day; it was not at all surprising to find that these soon became highly sought after collectors' items, and each edition sells out quickly. Unibic tell us that these tins 'celebrate the origin of the Anzac biscuit, reminding us of the packages of love and care from home that helped buoy the Anzac Spirit in the trenches of Gallipoli'.

Today, these striking tins represent more than just collectors' items. The tins and their contents are produced annually to commemorate significant events and the men and women who have served in or been affected by war. They stand as symbols of remembrance, and they are sold to raise funds and awareness for the Returned and Services League (RSL) Australia. In the past the company has produced biscuits and commemorative tins for New Zealand, UK, USA, Canada and India, supporting their respective servicemen's and veterans' associations.

Visiting the Modern Baking Company (MBC) in Melbourne

The enticing aroma of biscuit baking greets you as you arrive in the suburb of Broadmeadows, a short ride from Melbourne's Tullamarine airport. After donning the usual protective clothing and going through the screening process my brother David and I were taken to see the making and baking of the commercial Anzac biscuit. We were in awe of the sheer scale of the production – the sight of enormous piles of sugar and butter and the warm smell of golden syrup wafting around us as we watched piped biscuits disappear along a production line and into the longest oven tunnel I have ever seen. Every biscuit is timed to come out baked to perfection. At the factory the full collection of commemorative tins is proudly displayed in bookcases along the executive corridors of MBC.

Browsing the company archives, we discovered that Anzac

biscuits have been commercially manufactured by MBC (as Unibic) since 1998 when the company developed a relationship with the RSL, donating four per cent of the revenue from the sales to veterans through the RSL.

The year 2015 marked the centenary of Gallipoli, where the Anzac legend began; this was a special year for all Australians and New Zealanders, and to acknowledge it MBC released several commemorative tins for Anzac Day, 25 April. I was honoured to be invited to write the section entitled 'Something from Home' for the Anzac leaflet to be included in the tin commemorating the Australian Comforts Fund. It shows a montage of photographs of women at home proudly displaying

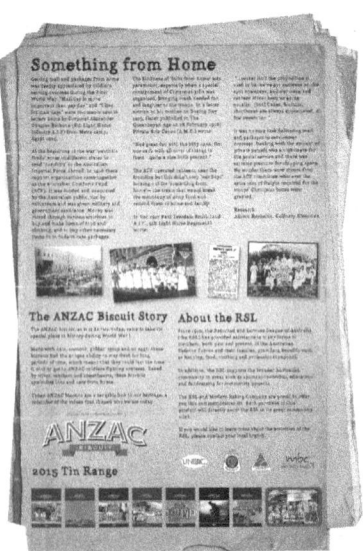 

Australian Comforts Fund commemorative Anzac biscuit tin with information leaflet produced for the Anzac Centenary by Unibic at the Modern Baking Company, Melbourne, 2015.

goods destined for care packages, women marching under the Australian Comforts Fund banner, and hundreds of crates piled high on a wharf waiting to be shipped overseas. These evocative images also include one of a newspaper cutting that announces 'Comforts Arrive at ANZAC – The First Contingent'; this would have provided much-needed good news.

This special commemorative Anzac biscuit tin is now destined to take pride of place among my biscuit tin collection. I feel sure Herbie and my other flatmates would approve.

Chapter 11
Sutton Veny to South Australia

'Though far away – not forgotten' – letters from No. 2 Camp
Picture this: it is April 2015, the height of the Anzac Centenary commemorations in Australia. I am quietly sitting in the Stirling library's history centre, browsing exhibits of local Anzac stories and memorabilia proudly displayed by the Mount Lofty Districts Historical Society. Carol Moore, secretary of the society, alerts me to a large photo album with a sepia photograph of a young soldier on the cover. This hefty document (a Year 9 school assignment) presented by Heathfield High School student Jesse Maker (age 14), contained several handwritten letters sent from Sutton Veny No. 2 Camp.

What a find! I started this Anzac biscuit story with a Sutton Veny connection and now, as I finish it, I return there with the discovery of these letters home. They were written by Jesse's great-great-great uncle, Samuel Roy Hocking (Roy), who fought and died in WWI.

During the few weeks Roy spent living on the edge of the exposed and desolate Salisbury Plain in the small Wiltshire village of Sutton Veny, he corresponded with his sister Myrtle and brother-in-law Bill back home in Wallaroo, on the Yorke Peninsula of South Australia. Roy was stationed at Sutton Veny No. 2 Camp from 7 November 1917 until 6 January 1918. Barely

In April 2015, Jesse Maker created this scrapbook of WWI letters, written by his great-great-great-uncle, Samuel Roy Hocking.

eight weeks. His letters reveal that it was a very cold winter.

The soldiers struggled to keep warm; cold winds from the north-east were bitter, especially when it rained. Roy was fascinated by the falling snow. He noticed that when it snowed it was not as cold and on rare occasions the sun would come out. All the big dams froze over and they had fun skating on them. However, Roy was fed up with camp life, especially standing in the cold on battalion drill for two hours every day. He was eager to be on his way to France. In every letter he sent home, Roy asked after the baby (his niece) who he called 'Little Jean'. Little Jean would grow up to have a son, Kevin Patterson, who is Jesse's grandfather.

Inspired by his grandson's Anzac project, Kevin joined the search and continued to research the records of the National Archives of Australia, Trove (Early Australian newspapers) and other sources. This culminated, in 2015, with the publication of Kevin's book on the family's WWI connections: *My Grandmother's Brother: Samuel Roy Hocking, a World War One Soldier.*

Anzac Biscuits

Sutton Veny
No.2 Camp
Dec 2 1917

Dear Bill & Myrtle
    Just a few lines to let you know that Im doing well and enjoying good health hoping this letter finds you the same well this an answer to the letter you wrote on Sept 27th which I was very pleased to hear from you and that you are doing hoping this letter finds you the same. Well Sister it's very cold over here at present and very wet we had some snow over here last week its not so cold when its snow but when its raining and the north east wind blow then its cold we put all the clothes on we can then we can't keep warm. Well I have seen some of them and had a good talk with them you know Duke (Elpick) Elphick well he has been married over here I met him in Warminster one Sunday afternoon that where we are camped now its much warmer than Larkhill I have not seen Clarrie yet and I will be going to France at the end of the month so if I don't see him before I go I may not see him for a long

copied as written by Roy
Duke Elphick is Alfred william Elphick from Wallaroo
Clarrie is Clarence Roy Bishop, Roy's uncle (his mum's brother)

Dec 2nd 1917

time he is not in the same Batt as me but I would like to see him before I go over the pond well one thing I'll see Ben when I get over to France and the sooner there the sooner back to good old Australia and to the best girl in the world well Bill I have received two cards which you sent me and they are very nice and I'll be sweet 20 tomorrow so it wouldn't be a bad plan to put in for a weeks leave I only came back from four days leave last Tuesday night I went to Bristol and it is a better place than London of London not bad if any one as never been there before but I have so I did not trouble about going there again well Sister this is all the news this time so I'll close with my love to you both.

                        I remain
I send my love to the xxx   Your loving
baby and these kisses xxx   Brother
hoping she is doing well xxx   Roy
                     xxx   xxxxxxxxxxxx
                                xxxxxxxxxxxx
Though far away not forgotten

Copied as written by Roy
Ben is brother in law to Roy and Myrtle
Letter written one day before his 20th birthday
Born 3rd December 1897

A montage of Roy Hocking's Sutton Veny No. 2 Camp letters (one of the letters is headed with military insignia), written between 2 December 1917 and 6 January 1918.

Sutton Veny to South Australia

Sutton Veny
No.2 Camp
Jan 6. 1917
(1918)

Dear Bill & Myrtle
              I now take the pleasure of writting you a few lines to let you know that Im doing well hoping this letter finds you the same Well today is the last day in England for a little while for we are going to France to our bit in this big war it just about time they sent us away for I am tired of this place. When we get over there I'll be able to see Ben and a few of the Wallaroo Boy there was lad over in France asking about me I cant make who it is he is in the 43rd Batt but I will soon see who it is. Well we are having very cold weather over here now plenty of snow it great fun out

Copied as written by Roy
Letter shows date as Jan 6th 1917 this should be Jan 6th 1918
Records show he left for France on Jan 8th 1918
Ben is his brother in law

in it after it as stopped when it is about two feet deep, but it pretty cold when there is a black frost everything on the ground get frozen and all the big dams are frozen they go skating on them and they make good skating rinks. Well this is all the new this time so I'll close with my love to you both and the baby.

        I remain
          Your Brother
            Roy
             xxxxx
             xxxx

Copied as written by Roy

Many moving Anzac stories like Jesse Maker's have come my way, sometimes through a chance conversation, sometimes when friends, family or strangers ask, 'Have you come across this?' I am indebted to many people. My biggest challenge came when I had the idea of sending 250 homemade Anzac biscuits to Sutton Veny Primary School as a way of connecting them with Australia on the centenary of Anzac Day. I discovered that students of the local Bridgewater Primary School and their teachers were also planning an Anzac Centenary commemoration. I wondered if this could become a joint project.

Bridgewater Primary School – strengthening the Anzac connection

I was delighted when Bridgewater Primary School principal Barb Jenkins, staff members Shaun Klingbiel and Liz Sanderson, and students from classes 4, 5 and 6 (known as Studio 34) saw this proposal as complementing their own Anzac Centenary project and enthusiastically embraced the opportunity to make a connection with Sutton Veny Primary School.

Students from Studio 34 had been learning about WWI and the ANZACs, the design and significance of memorials, and had been researching local servicemen from Bridgewater. Theirs is an ambitious project and includes building a war memorial to create a significant place of remembrance for the community. At the time, Studio 34 were also rehearsing for a performance to the school community inspired by the children's book *Anzac Biscuit* written by Phil Cummings and illustrated by Owen Swan.

Everyone understood that baking Anzac biscuits and making the connection with Sutton Veny School in this Anzac Centenary year was a way to thank them for the commemorations they

Bridgewater Primary School students Demelza Metha and Lucy Fisher-Hackett show off their culinary skills with volunteer Ellie McAllister.
(Adelaide Hills *Courier*, Anzac Day special, 2015.)

Volunteers and students from Bridgewater Primary School assist the author in packing the Anzac biscuits to be posted to Sutton Veny School, 2015.

undertake every Anzac Day. Luckily there was no shortage of volunteers to help. Combining two classes meant there were 60 students coming through the teaching kitchen on baking day. Hundreds of Anzac biscuits were made with the best stored for sending to Sutton Veny. Back in the classroom, students composed their individual letters to include in the packages along with photos of the students baking.

Adelaide Hills food company Emmaline's Country Kitchen kindly provided the necessary packaging to keep the biscuits fresh and prevent breakages. The cost of the postage – we did send them airmail – was generously met by Hahndorf Lions Club.

Local journalist Lisa Pahl spent time with the students and ensured that this remarkable Bridgewater Primary School/Sutton Veny Primary School story took pride of place in the special Anzac Day supplement of the *Courier*, the newspaper of the Adelaide Hills region (22 April 2015).

'Proud to Remember'

Every year the *Warminster Journal* covers the Anzac commemorations held throughout the local Wiltshire villages. In 2015 'Proud to Remember' was the bold headline referring to Sutton Veny Primary School. This sub-heading expressed the sentiment of the occasion:

> As part of its proud and longstanding ANZAC link Sutton Veny Primary School held its annual service on Friday, particularly poignant this year as it marked the centenary of the Gallipoli landings.

The newspaper report went on to say that the school had

welcomed a group of students from Southern Australia on a Connecting Spirits tour and also received biscuits baked by pupils at Bridgetown (sic) School in Australia. It was nice to get a mention and I'm sure we can forgive the local paper for not getting the school name right. The Sutton Veny students would have been busy making a 'Field of Remembrance' (a display of 100 willow poppies to commemorate 100 years), creating posies for each student to place on an ANZAC grave, and organising the commemoration service, under the guidance of Anzac coordinator Mrs Nicky Barnard. One can imagine the pleasant surprise that staff and students experienced just before Anzac Day when they received the large parcel from Australia. The letters back said it all.

Replies from England

Staff and students at Bridgewater Primary School were delighted when they received personal letters from the English children, the Sutton Veny teachers having matched the students and their interests well. The students wrote about their pets, their favourite sports and activities as well as the books they were reading and the computer games they were playing.

Some students wrote about what Anzac meant to them in their tiny country village school. Many of the letters were decorated with colourful drawings depicting Anzac symbols (crosses, poppies and even Anzac biscuits). Several students mentioned how happy they were at their small village school and how much they liked their teachers.

Included was a letter from head teacher Rachael Brotherton, expressing 'heartfelt gratitude' for the letters and Anzac biscuits. She wrote:

'Sutton Veny pupils pay tribute 100 years after Gallipoli landings'.
(*Wiltshire Times*, England, 25 April 2015. Photographer Glen Phillips)

Our children thoroughly enjoyed reading your letters and have sent their replies. The biscuits were delicious and we were overwhelmed at the time and care you took to send these all the way to us.

Miss Brotherton finished her letter by saying how proud Sutton Veny School was of their Anzac legacy and traditions and how much this had been strengthened by connecting with an Australian school such as Bridgewater Primary.

The Bridgewater students sent Sutton Veny students poetry that they penned during their studies on the First World War. These poems were very well received by the school community.

'Friends and Family' poem by Millie Tucker; 'Battle field' poem by Millie G.; and 'Anzac Biscuits' poem by Isabelle B. and Isabelle O. were all written at Bridgewater Primary School, Adelaide Hills, in 2015.

For almost 30 years (1939–1967) the famous First World War poet Siegfried Sassoon, who wrote of the futility of war, lived in the nearby village of Heytesbury. No doubt Sassoon was saddened by the many Wiltshire villages containing war graves of servicemen and women who had survived the Great War only to succumb to the Spanish flu while waiting to be repatriated home. But I'm sure he would have approved wholeheartedly of the students writing poetry. I wonder what he would have made of a humble oat biscuit later becoming associated with the Australian and New Zealand soldiers who fought at Gallipoli?

My amazing story has identified that Anzacs are indeed extraordinary everyday biscuits and that they still mean so much, more than a century after Gallipoli. In connecting young people in schools across the world, a new generation are sharing thoughts, ideas, memories – and Anzac biscuits.

Bibliography

'About Modern Baking.' Modern Baking Company, accessed 24 November 2014. http://www.modernbaking.com.au/about-us.html.

Alexander, Stephanie. *The Cook's Companion*. Ringwood, Victoria: Viking, 1996.

Anchor Ann's Recipe Book. Adelaide: G. Wood, Son & Co. Ltd, pre-1924 and 1925, p. 43.

'Anzac biscuits.' A short play adapted from the book by Phil Cummings and Owen Swan. Performed by students of Studio 34, Bridgewater Primary School, Adelaide Hills, 25 May 2015, 14 and 15 December 2016.

'Anzac Biscuits or Crispies.' Kitchen and Pantry, *Argus* (Melbourne), 15 September 1920, p. 7.

Anzac Centenary Commemoration Exhibition. Held at the History Centre, Coventry Library, by Mount Lofty Districts Historical Society, Stirling SA, April 2015.

Anzac Day Commemoration Committee. 'Anzac Biscuits' accessed 8 March, 19 July, 28 July 2013. http://www.anzacday.org.au/miscellaneous/bikkies.html.

'Anzac Day in Codford.' *Warminster Journal* (England), 1 May 2009, n.p.

'Anzac Day in Codford.' *Warminster Journal* (England), 6 May 2011, n.p.

'Anzac Day Service in Codford.' *Warminster Journal* (England), 14 July 2006, p. 5.

Armour, Jenny. 'ANZACS (Australian Cookies)' In *Biscuits Galore: W.I. Recipes*. UK: Women's Institute, n.p., n.d. Sent to Jenny in Darwin from Mother in UK between 1972 and 1975. Darwin, NT, personal communication, 2015.

Aunt Susan's recipes: a collection of tried and palatable dishes simple and economical. Adelaide: Vardon & Sons Ltd, 1920.

'Australia strikes a blow in the battle for the Anzac biscuit' http://www.theage.com.au/national/australia-strikes-a-blow-in-the-battle-for-the-anzac-biscuit-20140130-31oy8.html.

Australian Comforts Fund. *Australian Comforts Fund: Despatch of Food Parcels (private)*. Report of conference of delegates of the Australian Comforts Fund held in Sydney on 8 and 9 June 1917. Series: MP367/1, Item: 552/3/31 (Barcode: 365742). Melbourne: National Reference Service – National Archives of Australia, p. 48.

'Australian Comforts Fund (1916–1920)' *Trove*, National Library of Australia, Canberra, accessed 12 March 2014. http://trove.nla.gov.au/people/563480

Australian Government Department of Veterans' Affairs. 'Anzac Biscuit Recipe' accessed 24 March 2013. http://www.dva.gov.au/media.

Australian Government Department of Veterans' Affairs. 'Use of the Word Anzac' accessed 16 December 2014. http://www.dva.gov.au/commems_oawg/commemorations/protecting.

Australian War Memorial. 'Anzac biscuit: the origin and recipe' accessed 15 April 2007 http://www.awm.gov.au/encyclopedia/anzac/biscuit/recipe.htm.

'Australian Woman's Mirror' *Bulletin Newspaper* (Sydney), first published 1924, accessed 4 May 2014. http://trove.nla.gov.au/work/33657268?1-format=Periodical/Journal.

Back to Suttontown Recipe Book: Five Hundred Selected Recipes from the South East of South Australia. Mt Gambier, SA: Border Watch, 1933.

'Baked Relief sending love to the West in 2014' Online video, Food strategy Australia New Zealand Pty Ltd, accessed 12 April 2014. 2014foodstrategy.com.au/News/BlogNews/Releases/tab.

'Bake some relief this Anzac Day' *Queensland Country Life*, accessed 19 August 2015. http://www.queenslandcountrylife.com.au/news/agriculture/agribus.

Barnard, Nicky. Anzac Coordinator, Sutton Veny Primary School, Wiltshire, England, personal communications, 2007–2015.

Barossa Cookery Book: 400 Tried Recipes. Tanunda, SA: *Barossa News*, 1st edn, 1917. SLNSW 641.5/155, accessed 2013. email: imagingservices@sl.nsw.gov.au.

Barossa Cookery Book: Selected and Choice Recipes. 3rd edn Tanunda, SA: Tanunda Soldiers' Memorial, 1927.

'Battle of the Biscuit, every crumb counts in bid to solve Anzac mystery' *Advertiser* (Adelaide), 20 April 2013, p. 3.

Baulderstone, Yvonne. Adelaide Hills, personal communications, 2013–2014.

Baulderstone, Yvonne. 'Anzac biscuit recipe' In *Australian Women's Weekly: Big Book of Beautiful Biscuits*. 1st edn 1982, Paperback edition, Australian Consolidated Press, Sydney.

Bibliography

'Beechworth Red Cross Society' *Ovens and Murray Advertiser* (Beechworth, Vic.), 15 June 1918, accessed 30 May 2013. http:trove.nla.gov.au/nla.news-article.

Beeton, Isabella. *Mrs Beeton's Book of Household Management*. First published 1861, New Edition, London: Ward Lock, 1906.

Bethune, Alexander Douglas (Doug), 'B' Squadron, 8th Australian Light Horse Regiment, AIF. Letters from Egypt to Dolly in Melbourne, 20 July 1915. Collection held by his grand-niece Nicky Titchner, Adelaide SA, 2014.

Bethune, Norman McLeod, 8th Australian Light Horse Regiment, AIF. Letter from Anzac Cove to Dolly in Melbourne, 22 July 1915. Collection held by his grand-niece Nicky Titchner, Adelaide SA, 2014.

Bethune, Norman McLeod, 8th Australian Light Horse Regiment, AIF. Letters from Egypt to Dolly in Melbourne, 14 January 1917. Collection held by his grand-niece Nicky Titchner, Adelaide SA, 2014.

Bjelke-Petersen, Flo. *Classic Country Cooking: Traditional Australian Fare*. Melbourne: Mandarin Australia, 1992. Reprint, Melbourne: Reed Books Australia, 1994.

Black, Margaret. *Household Cookery and Laundry Work*. London and Glasgow: William Collins, 1890.

Bonnin, Irene. ANZAC Nurse. Diary entry 20 December 1915. Nurses' Letters and Diaries PRG621_21_Parcel.jpg. State Library of South Australia, accessed 20 November 2014.

Braithwaite, Robbie. 'The Kindness of Strangers' *Wartime: official magazine of the Australian War Memorial*, 18 (2002): p. 60.

Brinckman, Margaret. Archivist Department, Royal Hobart Show. The Royal Agricultural Society of Tasmania (RAST), Hobart, personal communication, 2014–2015.

Brotherton, Rachael. Sutton Veny Primary School, Wiltshire, England, personal communication, 2014–2015.

Brotherton, Rachael. Sutton Veny Primary School, Wiltshire, England. Letter to Bridgewater Primary School, Adelaide Hills, May 2015.

Brown, R. 5th ALTM Battery, 2nd Division, AIF. 'Orange Soldiers' Xmas Gifts: The First Acknowledgment' *Leader* (Orange, NSW), 30 January 1918, p. 1.

'Call to Arms – Anzacs for Anzac Day' Baked Relief with Baked Relief South Burnett. Accessed 11 April 2014. https://www.facebook.com/bakedrelief/posts/679212632135195:0.

Campbell, Mel. 'The Biscuiteer: Unibic Anzac Biscuit' The Enthusiast, accessed 19 November 2013. http://www.theenthusiast.com.au/archives/2009/the-biscuiteer-unib.

Capes, Erle. (AMC) Letter from Heliopolis to his mother in Queanbeyan, NSW, 26 December 1915. 'Our Boys in Kakki [sic]: Letters from the Front' *Queanbeyan Age and Queanbeyan Observer* (NSW), 18 February 1916, p. 3.

Carey, Caitlin. 'English village continues to remember its Anzac sons' *Courier* (Adelaide Hills), 21 April 2010, n.p.

Carson, Bronnie. ANZACS ... handwritten family recipe, Darwin, 1991.

Caulfield, 'Biscuits and Puddings' Kitchen and Pantry, *Argus* (Melbourne), 6 July 1921, n.p.

'Caulfield sends recipes asked for recently by correspondents: – Anzac Biscuits' *Argus* (Melbourne), 6 July 1921, p. 13.

Christmas, C.R. 5 Field Ambulance, AIF. 'Army biscuit Christmas card' accessed 4 November 2013. http://www.awm.gov.au/collection/REL/00918.

Clark, John. Section Coordinator, Perth Royal Show. Royal Agricultural Society of Western Australia (RASWA), personal communication, 2015.

'Comforts Arrive At ANZAC: The First Contingent' *Barrier Miner* (Broken Hill, NSW), 14 November 1915, 2, accessed 30 May 2013. http://trove.nla.gov.au/nla.news-article45344404.

Concise English Oxford Dictionary. 11th edn 2004.

Connecting Spirits Tour. April 2015. www.connectingspirits.com.au.

Cookery Book of Good and Tried Receipts. Compiled for the Women's Missionary Association of the Presbyterian Church of New South Wales. First published Sydney, 1895. 14th edn Sydney: Angus and Robertson, 1915.

Cookery Book of Good and Tried Receipts. Compiled for the Women's Missionary Association of the Presbyterian Church of New South Wales. First published Sydney, 1895. 19th edn Sydney: Angus and Robertson, 1927.

Courtney, Pip. Reporter. 'Kitchen Kindness' *Landline* ABC TV, 23 March 2014. http://www.abc.net.au/landline/content/2014/s3969450.htm.

Crismani, Danielle. Baked Relief Founder, accessed 20 October 2015. www.bakedrelief.org.

Cummings, Phil and Owen Swan (Illustrator). *Anzac biscuits*. Lindfield, NSW: Scholastic Press, 2013.

Daish, Lois. 'In Anzac Day by Fiona Rae' *New Zealand Listener*, July 1994, revisited in 2000, accessed 29 July 2014. http://www.listener.co.nz/lifestyle/food/recipes/anzac-biscuit-1994-2000.

Darian-Smith, Kate and Sara Wills. *Agricultural Shows in Australia – A Survey*. Melbourne: University of Melbourne, 1999, accessed 18 June 2015, State Library of South Australia, 630.60994D218.

Bibliography

Davidson, Alan. *The Penguin Companion to Food*. 2nd edn London: Penguin Books, 2002.

'Daybreak Service Honours Anzacs' *Warminster Journal* (England), 3 May 2013, p. 11.

Deverall, Tara and Kristy Skopp. Competition and Events Coordinators, Royal Queensland Show. Royal National Agricultural and Industrial Association of Queensland (RNA), Brisbane, personal communication, 2014–2015.

Digger History. 'Anzac Biscuits: aka Soldiers' biscuits' accessed 8 March 2013, 24 July 2013. http:// www.diggerhistory.info/pages-food/anzac-biscuits.htm.

Edmonds Sure to Rise Cookery Book. New Zealand: Edmonds Baking Powder Company, 1907.

Families and Friends of the First AIF Inc. 'Dawn Service UK' Posted 20 May 2008. Accessed 29 December 2014. http://fffaif.org.au/?p=248.

Farlam, David. 'Researching military records' Port Lincoln, SA, personal communication, 2014.

Farlam, Elizabeth (Beth). Antique and Antiquarian Cookery Book Collector, Adelaide Hills SA, personal communication, 2013–2015.

Folker, Christine. Sutton Veny Primary School, Wiltshire, England, personal communication, 2007.

'Fourth Prize for Anzac Ginger Biscuits' *Sunday Times* (Perth), 4 June 1916, p. 7.

Fulton, Margaret. *The Margaret Fulton Cookbook*. London; Sydney: Hamlyn, 1968.

Galletly, Duncan. Member, Food History Group of New Zealand, Dunedin, New Zealand, personal communication, 2013.

Glasse, Hannah. *The Art of Cookery Made Plain and Easy by a Lady*. First published 1747, Facsimile of the 1st edn, London: Prospect Books, 1983.

Green and Gold Cookery Book: containing many good and proved recipes. 1st edn, Adelaide: Vardon, 1924.

Grigson, Jane. *English Food*. London: Macmillan, 1974.

Hackett, Lady. *The Australian Household Guide*. Perth, WA: E.S. Wigg & Sons, 1916.

Hamill, Pam. Chief Steward, Cookery Section, Royal Darwin Show. Royal Agricultural Society of the Northern Territory (RASNT), personal communication, 2014–2015.

Harfull, Liz. Adelaide, personal communication, 2013.

Harfull, Liz. *The Blue Ribbon Cookbook*. Adelaide: Wakefield Press, 2008.

Heysen, Sallie. Sallie Heysen's Recipe Collection. The home of Hans Heysen, The Cedars, Hahndorf, South Australia, accessed 2012.

Hocking, Samuel Roy. Letters to Myrtle and Bill Moore, Wallaroo, Yorke Peninsula, SA, from Sutton Veny No. 2 Camp, 1917–1918. Collection accessed through Kevin Pattison, Adelaide Hills, personal communication, 2015.

Horwood, Andrew. Emmaline's Country Kitchen, Lobethal, Adelaide Hills, personal communication, April 2015.

Howard, John. Prime Minister, Canberra, Australia. Letter to Ms Christine Folker, Sutton Veny Primary School, Wiltshire, England, 31 March 2007.

Hoyle, John. *An Annotated Bibliography of Australian Domestic Cookery Books 1860–1950*. Willoughby, NSW: Billycan Cook, 2010.

Hughes, Miss Gwen. *Perfect Cooking: A Comprehensive Guide to Success in the Kitchen*. Birmingham, UK: Parkinson Stove Company, circa 1937.

Hyam, Kirsten. 'Julie's Anzac Day book a personal pilgrimage' *Courier* (Adelaide Hills), 17 April 2013, p. 18.

Jeanette, (Yarrawonga). 'Recipes Wanted' Kitchen and Pantry, *Argus* (Melbourne), 22 June 1921, n.p.

Jenkins, Barbara. Principal, Bridgewater Primary School, Adelaide Hills, personal communication, 2015.

Johnson, H. *The Home Treasure: Comprising Household Hints & Recipes and Health, Motor & Wireless Notes*. Adelaide: Eric J. Ames, 1930.

Johnston, Alexa. *Ladies a Plate: Traditional Home Baking*. New Zealand: Penguin Books, 2008.

Jones, Esther May and Mavis Jean Wright. Show Cooking Judges, Mount Gambier and SA Region. Family handwritten recipe book. Collection held by daughter Heather Say, Mount Gambier, SA, emailed 2013.

Josephine, E. (Brunswick). 'Anzac Biscuit or Crispies recipe' Kitchen and Pantry, *Argus* (Melbourne), 15 September 1920, p. 7.

Kennedy, Ann-Marie. 'Marketing's Influence on the Food Culture of a Nation: As told through the Edmonds Cookery Book' Conference on Historical Analysis & Research in Marketing (CHARM), Auckland University of Technology, New Zealand, 2011.

Kent, Michael and Audrey. 'Anzac Biscuits' From Mrs Simkins' Country Kitchen, the *Dalesman* (Yorkshire), August 2014, p. 38. Adelaide, personal communication, 2014.

Keogh, Melissa. 'Soldier's Family Keeps History Alive' *Courier* (Adelaide Hills), 17 June 2015, p. 3.

Bibliography

Kight, Julia. 'Anzac biscuit Recipe' From *Edmonds Sure to Rise Cookery Book*. New Zealand: Edmonds Baking Powder Company, 1989. Hawkes Bay, New Zealand, personal communication, 2013.

Kitchiner, M.D. William. *The Cook's Oracle: Containing Receipts For Plain Cookery*. First published 1822, 5th edn Edinburgh and London: A. Constable, 1823.

Klingbiel, Shaun. Teacher, Studio 34, Bridgewater Primary School, Adelaide Hills, personal communication, 2015–2016.

Kookaburra Cookery Book of Culinary and Household Recipes and Hints, collected and arranged by the Committee of the Lady Victoria Buxton Girls' Club. Adelaide: Frearson's Printing House, 1911.

Leach, Helen M. Anthropology Dept, University of Otago, New Zealand, personal communication, 2013.

Leach, Helen M. 'Anzac Biscuits – notes from an address to the New Zealand Guild of Foodwriters' Conference 1999.' Anthropology Dept, University of Otago, New Zealand, personal communication, 2013.

Leach, Helen M. 'Do Food Writers Set Food Traditions in Stone? and Other Thoughts on the Roles of Food Writers and Chefs in Moulding Cuisines' *Pen and Palate*, (NZ Guild of Food Writers), March (2000): pp. 14–17.

Linn, Rob. *Sharing the Good Earth, 175 Years of Influence and Vision*. Adelaide: Royal Agricultural & Horticultural Society of South Australia, March 2014.

Love, J.R.B. 14th Australian Light Horse Regiment, AIF. Letters from Egypt to family in Strathalbyn, SA, 1916–1918. Collection held by SLSA, PRG 214 series 39.

Lush, Eilleen. 'Anzac recipes' Queensland, personal communication, May 2014.

Lydeamore, Judith. Social Historian. Adelaide Hills, SA, personal communication, 2013–15.

Maclurcan, Mrs Hannah. *Mrs Maclurcan's Cookery Book: A Collection of Practical Recipes, Specially Suitable for Australia*. Townsville: T. Willmett, 1898.

Maker, Jesse. Year 9 Heathfield High School student. Assignment (scrapbook) exhibited in the Anzac Centenary Commemoration Exhibition, held at the Coventry Library by Mount Lofty Districts Historical Society, Stirling SA, April 2015.

Mason, Laura and Catherine Brown. *The Taste of Britain*. London: Harper Press, 2006.

McAdam, Isabel Elizabeth. Family handwritten recipe book, Penola, South Australia: from 1909. Collection held by Judy and Bill Thomas, South Australia, accessed April 2013.

McLachlan, Robin, Anthea Bundock and Marie Wood. 'Discovering Gallipoli: Research Guide' Bathurst, NSW: Australian War Memorial, 1990, p. 58.

McNeill, F. Marian. *The Scots Kitchen: Its Traditions and Lore with Old-Time Recipes*. London and Glasgow: Blackie and Son Ltd, 1929. Reprint 1930.

Monfries, Annie. Handwritten 'John Bull Oat Biscuits' recipe Wentworth, NSW, circa 1919. Collection passed to Annie's daughter Peggy Walton, Adelaide Hills, now held by Annie's granddaughter Jenny Fox, Strathalbyn, SA, personal communication, 2012.

Moore, Carol. Secretary, Mount Lofty Districts Historical Society, History Centre, Coventry Library, Stirling SA, personal communication, April 2015.

Noble, Miss Emily. *The Parkinson Cookery Book*. Melbourne: Metropolitan Gas Company, 1937.

Olney, Kiri. 'Julie's living in the past' *Courier* (Adelaide Hills), 14 December 2011, p. 52.

O.N. (Mornington). 'Quickly Made Biscuits' Kitchen and Pantry, *Argus* (Melbourne), 22 November 1916, n.p.

Pahl, Lisa. 'Traditional treat a surprise gift to English pupils' *Courier* (Adelaide Hills), 22 April 2015, p. 16.

Parson, Anne. 'Anzac biscuit recipe' In *Australian Women's Weekly Cookbook*. Sydney: Australian Consolidated Press, n.d. Adelaide Hills, personal communication, 2013.

Pattison, Kevin. *My Grandmother's Brother: Samuel Roy Hocking, A World War One Soldier*. Self-published, Adelaide Hills, July 2015.

Pennington, Cate and Elisabeth Grace. Archive Coordinators, Royal Sydney Easter Show. Royal Agricultural Society of New South Wales (RASNSW). Sydney, personal communication, 2014–2015.

Petho, Victoria. Private Victor Offe's granddaughter, Torrensville, SA, personal communication with Judith Lydeamore, July and August 2013.

P.L. (Semaphore). 'Make Anzac biscuit with easy recipe' What's Your Problem? *Advertiser* (Adelaide), 1 July 2014, n.p.

Plummer, Jennene. 'Cooking class, How to make ... Anzac biscuits' *Australian Woman's Day*, Sydney, Bauer Media group, n.d. p. 68. www.womansday.com.au

'Poignant Anniversary For Cap Badge Clean' *Warminster Journal* (England), 14 July 2006, p. 5.

Preston, Matt. 'Soldier on' Columnist, The Source, (Woolworths) *Good Taste*, FPC Magazines, April 2004, pp. 80–83. Photocopy Unibic. www.australiangoodtaste.com.au.

'Proud to Remember' *Warminster Journal* (England), 1 May 2015, p. 7.

Bibliography

P.W.M.U. Cookery Book of Victoria, compiled and issued by the Presbyterian Women's Missionary Union of Victoria. First published Melbourne 1916. 8th edn, Melbourne: Brown, Prior & Co. Ltd, 1927.

Rabbitt, Susan. Show Judge, Royal Adelaide Show. Interview. Adelaide: 28 July 2015.

Rabbitt, Susan. 'Anzac Biscuit Family Recipe' from Mother's (Winifred Ivy Phillips) family handwritten recipe book (Adelaide), circa 1930s. Collection now held by granddaughter Michailey McDonald, Adelaide, SA. Adelaide, personal communication, 2015.

'Red Cross Biscuits' *Goulburn Evening Penny Post* (NSW), 3 March 1930, p. 5.

Red Tractor Designs tea towel. 'Anzac Biscuit Recipe' accessed 2015. http://www.redtractor.com.au/general-store/tea-towels.

Reynolds, Allison. Culinary Historian, personal recollections. Adelaide, 2013–2016.

Reynolds, Allison. Tried and Tested – Crispy or Chewy Anzac Biscuit Recipe. Adelaide SA, 2013–2015.

Reynolds, Allison. 'Something from Home' Information leaflet for the Unibic 2015 Comforts Fund commemorative tin. Adelaide 2014.

Reynolds, Allison. 'Stir Up Memories' South Australian Cookbook Roadshow 2011–2013.

Richards, Annette. 'Ben's Anzac biscuit recipe' Found printed on a postcard, Hawkesbury Cruises, Sydney, NSW. www.hawkesburycruises.com.au. Melbourne, personal communication, 2015.

'Rolled Oat Biscuits' *Mail* (Adelaide), 10 August 1918, p. 11.

Rolled Oat biscuits 'Recipes' *Warwick Examiner and Times*, 9 March 1912, p. 9 http://nla.gov.au/nla.news-article82187155

Ross, Beth E., Myra G. Batchelor, Edith W.M. Kinnear and Helen S. Crossley. *School of Mines Cookery Book. Advertiser* (Adelaide), 1930.

Russell, George William Erskine. *Lady Victoria Buxton: A Memoir with Some Account of her Husband*. London: Longman Green and Co, 1919, p. 154.

Sanderson, Liz. Teacher, Studio 34, Bridgewater Primary School, Adelaide Hills, personal communication, 2015.

Santich, Barbara. *Bold Palates: Australia's Gastronomic Heritage*. Adelaide: Wakefield Press, 2012.

Sassoon, Siegfried. English poet, writer and soldier. Resident at Heytesbury House, Wiltshire, England, 1939–1967.

Schauer, Amy and Minnie Schauer. *The Schauer Cookery Book*. Brisbane: Edwards, Dunlop & Co. Ltd, 1909.

Seal, Graham. 'We're Here Because We're Here: Trench Culture of the Great War' *Folklore*, 124:2 (2013): pp. 178–199.

Shephard, Sue. *Pickled, Potted & Canned: How the Art and Science of Food Preserving Changed the World*. New York: Simon and Schuster, 2006.

'She's A Good Cook . . . Anchor Ann's kitchen in the All-Australian Exhibition' Advertisement, *Advertiser* (Adelaide), 28 March 1925, p. 12.

Shiell, Dr Annette. Curator, Heritage and Curator, Art, Craft and Cookery, Royal Melbourne Show. Royal Agricultural Society of Victoria (RASV), Melbourne, personal communication, 2014–2015.

Shore, Libby. 'My Anzac Biscuits' Member of Combined Hills History Group. Adelaide Hills, SA, personal communication, 2014.

Smith, Neil. 'Origin of the term Digger' In *Military History* accessed 20 November 2015. http://www.findmypast.com.au.

'Soldiers' Biscuits'. Albury Banner and Wodonga Express (NSW), 14 March 1930, p. 22.

'Soldier's War-biscuits' *Yea Chronicle* (Victoria), 10 February 1916, n.p. accessed 20 April 2013. http//trove.nla.gov.au/ndp/del/article/59956952?.

Southland Red Cross Cookery Book. Invercargill, New Zealand: Red Cross, 1916.

Spiers, Steven. President, Hahndorf Lions Club, Hahndorf, Adelaide Hills, personal communication, April 2015.

St Andrew's Cookery Book. Dunedin, New Zealand: St Andrew's Friendly Aid Society, 7th edn 1915, 8th edn 1919, 9th edn 1921.

'Supporting the RSL.' Unibic Anzac Biscuits, accessed 24 November 2013 and 24 November 2014. http://unibicanzacbiscuits.com.

Supski, Sian. 'Anzac Biscuits – A Culinary Memorial' In Constantino, Emma and Sian Supski (eds), *Culinary Distinction*, Special Issue of *Journal of Australian Studies*, 87 (2006): pp. 51–59.

Sutton Veny. '1st World War.' Accessed 27 August 2014. http://suttonveny.co.uk/1st world-war.

Sutton Veny Church of England Primary School. 'About Us' Accessed 27 August 2014. http://www.suttonveny.wilts.sch.uk/about-us/anzac.

Sutton Veny Primary School students. Wiltshire, England. Letters to Bridgewater Primary School students, Adelaide Hills, May 2015.

Symons, Michael. *One Continuous Picnic: A History of Eating in Australia*. Adelaide: Duck Press, 1982.

Symons, Michael. 'Australia's cuisine culture: a history of our food'. *Australian Geographic*, 27 June, 2014.

Symons, Michael. 'The Cleverness of the Whole Number': Social Invention in the

Bibliography

Golden Age of Antipodean Baking, 1890–1940. Petits Propos Culinaires 85, May 2008, 31–60.

'Taking the Biscuit' *Antiques Trade Gazette: The Art Market Weekly*, 2153, (2014): p. 18.

Tarlinton, Chris. Steward, Cookery Section, Royal Canberra Show. Royal National Capital Agricultural Show, Canberra, personal communication, 2015.

Taste.com.au. 'Anzac biscuit recipe' accessed 2015. www.taste.com.au/.../ anzac-biscuits/cc4e2031-8b63-48e7-8eff-b2637f47...

Teesdale Smith, Paul. 9th Australian Light Horse Regiment, 2nd AIF. Letters from Gallipoli to family in the Adelaide Hills, SA. n.d., 3 November 1915, 12 December 1916, 5 December 1917. Collection held by his grandson, Stewart Johnston, Sydney, NSW, 2014.

The Men of ANZAC. *The ANZAC Book: written and illustrated in Gallipoli by the men of ANZAC, for the benefit of Patriotic funds connected with A & NZAC.* London: Cassell, 1916.

Unibic. 'About Anzac Biscuits' accessed 18 July 2013. http://unibic anzacbiscuits.com/about-anzac-biscuits.html.

Unibic. 'Unibic Anzac Biscuit Tins' accessed 24 November 2014. http:// unibicanzacbiscuits.com/unibic-anzac-biscuit-tins.html.

'Useful Recipes' *Kapunda Herald* (South Australia), 31 January 1913.

'Village School Proud to Remember Anzacs' *Warminster Journal* (England), 3 May 2013, p. 10.

Vincent, Sue. 'Australian flapjack recipe' Family handwritten recipe book, UK: (circa 1950), accessed 2014.

Vine, Frederick T. *Biscuits for Bakers.* London: Hampton, 1896.

War Chest Cookery Book. Sydney: Websdale, Shoosmith, 1917. Photocopy, National Library of Australia, accessed 7 August 2013. http://nla.gov.au/ nla.aus-vn1955520-sl-v.jpg.

Ward, Marilyn. Archivist, Royal Adelaide Show. Royal Agricultural & Horticultural Society of South Australia (RAHS SA), personal communication, 2013–2015.

Warner, Caroline. Family handwritten recipe notebook, Nhill, Victoria, 1912. Collection held by granddaughter Carol Moore, Adelaide Hills, accessed 2013.

Weaver, Gilly. Co-director, ANZA Social Welfare, Jakarta. Interview, Adelaide, 15 July 2015.

Weaver, Gilly. 'Anzac biscuit recipe' From *Edmonds Sure to Rise Cookery Book.*

New Zealand: Edmonds Baking Powder Company, 1997. Adelaide, personal communication 2013.

Wehner, Kirsten. Curator National Museum of Australia. 'Conversation with Alan Saunders' *Saturday Morning Breakfast,* ABC Radio National, Australia, 23 April 2005.

White, Madison. 'Iconic biscuit has a convoluted history' Herald Lifestyle, *Weekender Herald* (Adelaide Hills), 17 April 2015, p. 24.

Whitelock, Carole. Presenter, *Afternoons 891,* ABC Radio Adelaide, April 2013.

Wilkinson, Simon. (Maggie Beer's Anzac biscuit recipe) 'Sweet Taste of Home' Taste, *Advertiser* (Adelaide), 22 April 2015, p. 32.

Williams, Tanya. 'Baked Relief Founder Danielle Crismani Created A Movement' In *Woman of Influence,* accessed 19 August 2015. http://www.woman.com.au/interview-with-baked-relief-founder-da.

Wiltshire Online Parish Clerk Project. 'History: Sutton Veny War Graves' Accessed 22 March 2015. http://www.Wiltshire-opc.org.uk.

Wolff, Jane. 'Jane's Gluten-Free Anzac Biscuits' Parent at Bridgewater Primary School, Adelaide Hills, personal communication, March 2015.

'Your Food, 3 new ways with Anzac biscuits' *Woman's Day.* Sydney: Bauer Media Group, April 2013, p. 40.

Yvonne. 'A Fund Raising Experiment: Recipe for Success' *Touchstone,* (the Methodist paper), 2 November 2012.

Online Videos

Cooking With Karma. 'Anzac Biscuits' accessed 2015. https://www.youtube.com/watch?v=DTsHMgOUSzo.

CSR Sugar Recipes. 'Giant Chewy Anzac Biscuits' Colonial Sugar Refining Company North Sydney, NSW, accessed 2015. http://www.csrsugar.com.au/csr-sugar/recipes/giant-chewy-anzac.

Good Chef Bad Chef. 'Anzac Cookies' accessed 2015. https://www.youtube.com/watch?v=gPso8OlscLg&t=10s.

Keep Calm and Bake. 'Anzac biscuit' accessed 2015. https://curiosity.com/paths/anzac-biscuits-keep-calm-and-bake-s08e4-8-videojug-food.

One Pot Chef. 'Anzac biscuits' accessed 2015. https://www.youtube.com/watch?v=txYXk-ANm0Y.

Puttock, Tobie. 'Jamie Oliver's Anzac Day Biscuits' accessed 2015. http//www.jamieoliver.com/ videos/anzac-day-biscuits-tobie-puttock.

Glossary

Buckshee: In the *Concise English Oxford Dictionary*, 11th edition, edited by Catherine Soanes and Angus Stevenson, buckshee is defined as 'free of charge. Origin First World War: alt. of BAKSHEESH'.

Digger: According to Neil Smith the term 'digger' probably first occurred in the Australian goldrush days of the 1850s. When the ANZAC soldiers landed at Gallipoli in 1915, historical documents state that the ANZAC leader William Birdwood was told 'having got through the difficult business of landing, now you only have to dig, dig, dig'. The term became synonymous with the Anzac's strength, mateship and bravery.

Acknowledgements

This book started as a culinary history project, the seed planted years ago when I revisited Sutton Veny Primary School. It's been a privilege to tell their story and to connect them with Bridgewater Primary School in South Australia. Thanks to the head teachers at Sutton Veny School, Christine Folker and Rachael Brotherton, and to their Anzac coordinator Nicky Barnard who has passionately cherished the Anzac legend.

When I heard that Bridgewater Primary School students were studying the First World War I decided to ask them for assistance. School principal Barbara Jenkins, teachers Shaun Klingbiel, Liz Sanderson and Heather Cranna, volunteers (especially Ellie McAllister), and the students of Studio 34 all made it happen. A big thank you to Andrew Horwood and Stephen Spiers for their much-needed support. A special thank you to Shaun for passing on the insightful students' poetry.

Thank you to the Anzac Centenary Local Grants Program and the Department of Veterans' Affairs for the small grant towards the publishing costs – it really did make a difference. For valuable assistance with the ACLGP grant submission thanks to Kym Brown, Ann Herraman, Carol Moore, Christian Reynolds, Paul Reynolds and Fiona Roberts. Thank you to the following organisations who supported my grant application: Adelaide Farmers' Market; Australian War Memorial; Heathfield High School; Modern Baking

Acknowledgements

Pty Ltd; Mount Lofty Districts Historical Society Inc.; Sutton Veny CE Primary School; The Returned & Services League of South Australia; The Returned & Services League of Australia Stirling Sub-Branch Inc.; The South Australian Country Women's Association Inc. and the University of Adelaide.

To boost the publishing funds and spread the word on my research I have given many talks, written articles and presented papers on the Anzac biscuit. Thank you to all the community groups involved. I was pleased to be able to share my research at both the Australian and the New Zealand Gastronomy Symposia and the University of South Australia, Traces of War Symposium. A special mention for additional financial support to the Crafers Walking Group; Modern Baking Company; Mount Lofty Districts Historical Society; Older Women's Advisory Committee (SA) and Sugar Australia Pty Ltd.

Chance conversations lead to precious family soldiers' letters. Sincere thanks to Nicky Titchner, J.H. Love, Stewart Johnson, Kevin Pattison and Jesse Maker.

A presentation at the State Library of South Australia alerted me to the collection of South Australian Anzac nurses' letters and diaries. Thank you David Bonnin and library staff for your help.

The following institutions have been essential to my research: Australian War Memorial; Barr Smith Library, University of Adelaide; Department of Veterans' Affairs, Canberra; Emily McPherson Library, Melbourne; Mitchell Library, Sydney; National Archives of Australia (Melbourne and Adelaide); National Library, Canberra, and Trove; the State Libraries of Queensland, South Australia and Victoria.

I am grateful to the public for supporting the SA Cookbook Roadshows. Viewing old published and community cookery books encouraged my interest in food history. For family handwritten recipe books, I am indebted to Geoffrey Bishop, Jenny Fox, Carole Moore, Mary Pulford, Heather and Stephen Say, and Judy and Bill Thomas. Homemade Anzac biscuits were baked for all presentations and I sincerely thank the bakers: Yvonne Baulderstone, Beth Farlam, Graham Phillips and Libby Shore.

A big thank you to local and national radio stations (especially ABC Adelaide and Carole Whitelock); Country Style Australia (Kylie Walker); History SA (Pauline Cockrill); SA newspapers and Sydney Living Museum (Jaqui Newling) for promoting my research.

Recipes for Anzacs, their precursors or similar biscuits, came from across the world. From Jenny Amour, Yvonne Baulderstone, Bronnie Carson, Estate of Hans Heysen, Pat Kaye, Michael and Audrey Kent, Jules Kight, Eilleen Lush, Diana McGregor, Anne Parsons, Lesley Phipps, Annette Richards, Libby Shore, Helen Storer, Sue Vincent, Gilly Weaver and Jane Wolff. Not all recipes featured, but I am thankful for them all.

Many people provided their early cookery books for research, thank you to Valmai Bellinger (Robin), Stroma Buttrose, Beth Farlam, Ronda Peach (Maggie Ragless collection), Adrienne Piggott, Margaret Reichardt, Robbie Seymour and Lynda Van Adrighem.

Staff and volunteers from the Royal Show Societies around Australia completed the questionnaire and provided information on special Anzac biscuit classes. Thanks to: the Royal Agricultural & Horticultural Society of SA Inc; the Royal Agricultural Society of NSW; the Royal Agricultural Society of Tasmania; the Royal Agricultural Society of Victoria; the Royal Agricultural Society of Western Australia; the Royal Canberra Show; the Royal Darwin Show; and the Royal National Agricultural and Industrial Association of Queensland. Special thanks to Marilyn Ward, Elisabeth Grace and Cate Pennington, Margaret Brinckman, Dr Annette Shiell, John Clark, Chris Tarlington, Pam Hamill, Tara Deverall and Kristy Skopp. Thank you, Susan Rabbitt, for sharing your show-judging expertise.

Thank you Duncan Galletly and the many New Zealand food historians who have contributed to this Anzac biscuit story and particularly Emeritus Professor Helen Leach (University of Otago) for generously sharing her early research.

Acknowledgements

Thank you to Gilly Weaver, Danielle Crismani and the Modern Baking Company for letting me share your inspiring Anzac biscuit stories. And thanks to Liz Harfull for her *Blue Ribbon Cookbook* Anzac story and expert author advice.

Michaela Andreyev, thank you for your invaluable publishing advice. Grateful thanks to Andrea Cross and friends for legal advice. Thank you to the team at Wakefield Press and especially my editor Julia Beaven.

Thanks to Emeritus Professor Barbara Santich who inspired my academic studies through the Le Cordon Bleu Master of Gastronomy at the University of Adelaide. Dr Barbara Wall, thank you for alerting me to the letters of Paul Teesdale Smith and for encouragement and friendship. Thanks to Beth Farlam for the use of her extensive cookery book collection, First World War memorabilia, 'antique roadshow' expertise, and her baking prowess; to Judith Lydeamore for outstanding research and encouragement; and David Farlam for the much-needed expertise on Anzac military history. Thanks to Nicki Agars, friend and neighbour, for your food styling skills and creative eye.

Thanks to Georgie Humphries for her photography skills and to my brother David Humphries for being my Melbourne chauffeur. Thanks also to my sister, UK artist Frankie Woods, for her valuable design and printing advice and her ingenious iPad drawings. To my good friend Annette Richards, thank you so much for your editing and indexing skills, your patience and attention to detail have been a blessing. Thanks to my son Christian for his computer skills and continual encouragement long after he left Adelaide for pastures new.

And special thanks to my husband Paul for seeing me through the many aspects of creating this book. I will now endeavour to relax and enjoy our lovely home and garden.

Index

A
ABC Radio 891 5, 74
Agars, Nicki 32
Alexander, Stephanie 83
Anchor Ann's Recipe Book 88–90
Anzac 30–31, 46
  centenary 103, 111–112, 122, 124, 128, 130
  Day vi, x, 2, 3, 5–6, 130–131
    Menu, Hotel Cecil, 1916 vi
  and Helles 30
  nurses WWI 64
  spirit 116–117, 121
  stories 124–128
  wafer or tile 40, 43, 45, 48, 50, 53
ANZAC ix, 29–30, 52
  acronym ix, 29–31
  cemeteries 1–6, 131, 134
  commemorations 111–112, 115, 124, 128–134
  legacy 6, 131–134
Anzac biscuits
  with almonds 76–78, 81, 95, 99
  baked by school children 5, 104, 113, 115, 128–134
  and coconut 81–83, 88–90, 95
  commemorative 55, 116, 122–123
  commercial production 121–122
  and crispies 34, 37, 39, 55, 92
  earliest published recipes 33–39
  and flapjacks 24–27
  gluten-free 103–104
  history 56, 58, 69, 70–71, 77–78, 95, 98, 115
  iced 35
  ingredients 9–10, 32, 40, 96–97
  key ingredients 10
  meaning and memory ix, x, 30–31, 117, 133–134
  method of making 7–9, 19, 32–34, 77, 96–97
  myths and legends x, 7, 55–56, 69, 71
  and national identity ix, 117
  origins 7, 18–22, 24–29, 32–33, 35–39, 42, 71, 115, 121
  recipes 9, 25–26, 29, 34–39, 70, 72, 74–77, 81–83, 89, 92–106
  Allison's tried and tested 96–97, 104
  and rolled oat biscuits 32, 34, 37, 55, 83
  as show cookery 91, 108–115
  shelf life 10
  variations 81, 95, 98–99, 102–103, 112
Anzac Book, The 48–49
ANZACs ix, 1–6, 30, 39, 53, 116, 122
  care packages ix, 46, 55–67, 121–123
  'iron' (emergency) rations 40, 43, 45, 52
  see also diggers, trench culture
Army biscuits 40–43, 48–49, 52–53
  as a Christmas card 52
  as souvenirs 52–53
  uses for 50, 52–53
Australia and New Zealand Association (ANZA) 118–119
Australian Household Guide 11–12, 22, 84, 88
Australian
  Comforts Fund (ACF) 56, 64–69, 122–123
  Imperial Forces 3, 42
    Chalk Army Badge, Codford 3–4
  newspaper recipes 22, 29, 33–35, 38, 75, 78–79, 90, 92–95
  war graves 1–3; *see also* ANZAC cemeteries
  War Memorial 95
  War Museum, Canberra 52
  women's league 65

B
Baked Relief 116–118
Barker, David 49
Barnard, Nicky 5, 131
Barossa Cookery Book 50–51, 54, 84
Baulderstone, Yvonne 82, 104
Beeton, Isabella 11–12, 17, 23
Bethune, Alexander Douglas 58–59, 61
Bethune, Norman McLeod 44, 58, 61, 66–67
Birdwood, William 30
biscuits
  Anzac ginger 33
  navy 41–42
  quick 32

Index

received in soldiers' parcels 58, 61–65, 68–69
rolled oat 32, 34, 36–37, 55, 94, 96–97, 110
ship's 40, 42
surprise 32, 83
see also army, brownies, flapjack, ginger, hardtack, jawbreakers, oatmeal, munchies, nutties, Red Cross, soldiers' biscuits
Biscuits for Bakers 41
Bjelke-Petersen, Flo 99
Black, Mary 19
Blue Ribbon Cookbook, The 115
Bonnin, Irene 64–65
bread
  pilot 40; ship's 41
Bridgewater Primary School 103, 128–133
  students' Anzac poems 132–133
broonie 15
Brotherton, Rachael 131–132
Brown, Catherine 13
Brown, R. 47–48
brownies 83
bully beef 42–45, 48–49, 61
Burton, O.E. 48
Buxton, Lady Victoria 12, 84, 86–87

C

cakes 11–12, 15–16, 117
  Afghans 119
  Anzac 37–38
  Belgian Coffee 73
  blow-away 109
  boiled fruit 28, 109, 111–112
  Coffee 31
  Gallipoli Tea Cake 31–32
  Genoa 109
  Land of 84, 86
  melting moments 119
  patriotic name changes 73
  received in soldiers' parcels 63, 66–68
  as show cookery 109
  Victoria sandwich 23, 107
  see also broonie, ginger, gingerbread, lamington, moggy, parlies
Capes, Erle 45–47
Carson, Bronnie 81–82
Charles, Lionel Bruce 53
Church
  Codford 3, 6
  Heytesbury 2

Sutton Veny 1, 2, 3
Christmas
  C.R. 52
  Fund, Princess Mary 1914 67
  in the trenches 47
Classic Country Cooking: Traditional Australian Fare 99
cocoanut 9, 26, 54, 77, 85, 88–90
coconut 9, 10, 24–25, 27, 32, 35, 38, 72, 81–85, 88–90, 95
  desiccated 81, 83–85, 96–97
  facts 83
  popularity 84
Codford 3–6
Coll, Miss (knitting) 68
Comforts parcels ix-x, 31, 46, 55–58, 62–69, 99
  see also ANZACs care packages
Commonwealth War Graves Commission 1–3
Connecting Spirits tour 131
Cookbook Roadshow, South Australia (SACRS) 70–71
Cookery Book of Good and Tried Receipts 84, 88
cookery books
  early Australian 9, 11–12, 14–17, 19, 22, 25–26, 31–32, 35–36, 39, 50–51, 54, 70–71, 76, 79, 84–90, 98
  early British 13–20, 25–26, 41
  early New Zealand 37–39, 98
  see also family handwritten recipe books and individual titles
Cook's Oracle, The 14–16
Crismani, Danielle 116–117
CSR (Colonial Sugar Refining Company) 102–103
Cummings, Phil 128

D

Daish, Lois 56
Darian-Smith, Kate 109
Davidson, Alan 15, 19, 24
Diggers ix, 31, 33, 43–48, 50–53, 111, 115
  letters 43–48, 50–51, 57–63
Discovering Gallipoli Research Guide 42

E

Edmonds Sure to Rise Cookery Book 98
eggs 7, 19, 28, 63, 71, 92
  rationing 10
Egypt, Australian troops in ix, 45–46, 59–60, 66
  Mena Camp 59–60

F
family handwritten recipe books 27, 31, 35, 38, 70–80, 83, 85, 106
Farlam, Beth 57, 67, 82, 104
Farlan, David 51
flapjack
  Australian 25–26
  British 24–29
Fox, Jenny 93

G
Galletly, Duncan 38
Gallipoli ix, 30–31, 42–43, 48–49, 52–53, 55, 58, 60, 62, 95, 111, 121, 122, 130, 132, 134
  centenary 103, 111–112, 122, 124, 128, 130
  tea cakes 31–32
ginger
  biscuits 11–13, 27–28, 34
  cake 11, 13
  fluff 109
gingerbread 7, 11–17, 21–22, 27–28
  Aboriginal Prize Recipe 76
Glasse, Hannah 16, 18
Grigson, Jane 20–21
golden syrup 8–12, 21–22, 28, 32, 34, 40, 76–77, 79, 96, 118–119
  tins 56–57
'gunfire' breakfast 3

H
Hackett, Lady 11–12, 22, 84
hardtack 40–45, 48–50, 52–53
Harfull, Liz 115
Hele, Ivor 3
Hewett, Otho 49
Heysen, Sallie 99
Heytesbury 2, 6, 107–108, 134
Hocking, Samuel Roy 124–127
Howard, John 5–6
Hughes, Gwen L. 25
Humphries, David 6, 121

J
jacks, Australian 25–27
jawbreakers 43, 50, 53
Jeanette of Yarrawonga 35, 92–93
Jenkins, Barb 128
Johnston, Alexa 98
Jones, Esther May 77–78
Josephine of East Brunswick 34, 92

K
Kennedy, Ann-Marie 98
Kent, Audrey and Michael 100
Klingbiel, Shaun 128
Kookaburra Cookery Book 11–12, 17, 19, 22, 84–87

L
Ladies, a Plate: Traditional Home Baking 98
lamingtons 54, 84, 90, 111, 119
'Land of Cakes' 84, 86
Lawson, Bob 95
Leach, Helen 37, 39, 55
Lemnos 46
Listener, New Zealand 56
Love, J.R.B. 45
Lydeamore, Judith 51

M
Maclurcan, Mrs 11, 12
Maker, Jesse 124–128
Mason, Laura 13, 19, 21
McAdam, Isabel Elizabeth 74–75, 77–80
  poem 80
McNeill, F. Marian 13–14
methods of making 7–9, 18–19
  creaming 8, 35
  melting 8–9, 11–14, 16, 22, 32–34
  rubbing in 8, 16
Modern Baking Company (MBC) 121–122
moggy 22
Monfries, Annie 93–94
Moore, Carol 71, 124
Mount Lofty Districts Historical Society 124
munchies 75–76, 78

N
Noble, Emily 25
nutties 83, 110

O
oatcake, Scottish 7, 19–21, 27–28
oatmeal 7, 15–22, 28
  biscuits 11, 17–20, 32
oats 7–10, 13, 17–22, 24–28, 32, 34–37
  John Bull 34–35, 92–94
  rolled 7, 9, 24, 32, 35–36, 40, 54, 96–98
Offe, Victor 50–51, 54
oven temperatures 17

P
Pahl, Lisa 130
parkin, 7, 11, 15, 21–22, 27–28
  treacle 22

Index

Parkinson Stove Company Ltd 25–26
parlies 13–14, 27–28
Patterson, Kevin 125
pavlova ix, 84, 98
Petho, Victoria 51
pickles 74, 76
poetry 79–80, 118, 132–134
puddings 23, 31, 44, 54–55, 74, 92–93
  Anzac 37;
  Cocoanut 77, 92
  War Time Plum 54
  pumpkin scones 84, 99, 109
PWMU Cookery Book of Victoria 31–32, 84

Q
Quaker Oat Company 19, 20
Queensland, floods and drought 116–117

R
Rabbitt, Susan 104–106, 114
Ralston, Mary 35
recipes for Anzac biscuits
  Allison Reynolds' tried and tested 96–97, 104
  in Australian newspapers 22, 29, 33–35, 38, 75, 78–79, 90, 92–95
  on YouTube 101–102
Red Cross biscuits 33, 58, 75–78, 83
Rice, Maureen 5
Ross, Beth E. 25
RSL x, 115, 121–122

S
Sanderson, Liz 128
Santich, Barbara ix, 7, 28, 56, 83–84
Sassoon, Siegfried 134
Say, Heather and Stephen 77–78
Schauer Cookery Book, The 84
School of Mines Cookery Book 25–26
Scottish Parliament cake 13–14, 27–28
Seal, Graham 52
Shephard, Sue 40–41
Shore, Edith 56
Shore, Libby 100–101
show cooking 77, 107–115
  and Anzac Centenary 111–113
  judges 77, 91, 104, 106, 113–114
  trends in baking 109, 112
shows, agricultural
  history 109–110
  Perth Royal 111
  Royal Adelaide 108, 113–114
  Royal Canberra 111
  Royal Darwin 110, 114–115
  Royal Melbourne 112–114
  Royal Queensland 114
soldiers' biscuits 33, 58, 78–79, 83
Southland Red Cross Cookery Book 37
St Andrews Cookery Book 37–39
Sunderland gingerbread nuts 12–13
Supski, Sian 11, 56–57
Sutherland, Mrs M. 33
Sutton Veny 1–6, 124–128, 130
  Primary School 1, 2, 5, 128–132
  Anzac connection 5–6
  No 2 Camp 124–127
Swan, Owen 128
Symons, Michael 84

T
Teesdale Smith, Paul 43–44, 62–63
Thomas, Bill and Judy 74
tins
  collectors' biscuit 116, 120–123
  commemorative 120–123
  golden syrup 56–57
  Princess Mary Christmas Fund 67
  Yorkshire pudding 23
Touchstone, New Zealand Methodist newspaper 38
trench/es
  life in the 42, 47–54
  porridge 50–51, 54

U
Unibic 120–122
Usni 119–120

V
Vincent, Sue 26
Vine, Frederick T. 41

W
Waitaki butter 37–38
War Chest Cookery Book 35–37
War Chest Fund, Sydney 35, 65
Warner, Caroline Sarah 71–73, 77, 79
Weaver, Gilly 118–119
Whitelock, Carole 5
Wilkinson, Simon 103
Wills, Sara 109
Woods, Frankie 6
Wright, Mavis Jean 77

Y
Yorkshire pudding 23
Yorkshire 'Th: hearth' cake 15, 16

Wakefield Press is an independent publishing and
distribution company based in Adelaide, South Australia.
We love good stories and publish beautiful books.
To see our full range of books, please visit our website at
wakefieldpress.com.au
where all titles are available for purchase.
To keep up with our latest releases, news and events,
subscribe to our monthly newsletter.

Find us!

Facebook: facebook.com/wakefield.press
Twitter: twitter.com/wakefieldpress
Instagram: instagram.com/wakefieldpress

www.ingramcontent.com/pod-product-compliance
Lightning Source LLC
Chambersburg PA
CBHW071004160426
43193CB00012B/1916